Healthy Habits
for a Better Life

よりよい健康生活を求めて

Joan McConnell   Kiyoshi Yamauchi

SEIBIDO

photographs by

iStockphoto

Sabrana Hydol

Healthy Habits for a Better Life

PREFACE

Dear Students,

Did you know that selecting an interesting and informative theme is the most challenging part of preparing a textbook?

Last November when I was in Tokyo, I met with my co-author Professor Kiyoshi Yamauchi and our Seibido editor Mr. Takashi Kudo. After lengthy discussions, we decided that the theme of our new book would be how healthy habits make our lives better. After all, everybody wants to be healthy!

Healthy Habits for a Better Life has 15 chapters, each of which includes six parts to help improve your English skills.

Part One contains a **Vocabulary Gallery** of six words, sample sentences and a short exercise.

Part Two presents the **Warm-up Dialogue** where the chapter theme is introduced in colloquial, informal English. The **Multiple Choice Questions** serve as a short comprehension check-up.

Part Three is **Ready to Read.** Here the author discusses the chapter topic in clear, direct English along with helpful notes in Japanese by Prof. Yamauchi. The **Comprehension Check-up** and **Guided Summary** test your understanding of the reading passage. Finally you can enjoy the **Did You Know?** section in Japanese.

Part Four is **Language Highlights** where Prof. Yamauchi explains key words and constructions used in the reading passage. He has also added **Grammar Practice** exercises.

Part Five is the **Slash Reading Challenge.**

Part Six is **Let's Talk about It.** Please have fun discussing these interesting topics with your partners.

In conclusion, Professor Yamauchi and I hope that our book will encourage you to understand how and why healthy habits can help you have a better life.

All my best to you for a happy, harmonious and healthy future,

Dr. Joanie McConnell

多くの優良テキストの中から、本書をお選びいただき誠にありがとうございます。

このテキストを英語学習の良き友としてご活用いただければ、やさしい語彙で書かれてはいながらも、非常にこなれた英文を読みながら、英文法の基礎を復習し、練習問題を通じ総合的な英語力を伸ばしつつ、大学生としてふさわしいレベルの健康トピックについて学び、さらに教養も身につけていただけるものと確信いたします。練習問題には様々な工夫を凝らし、学習効率が高まるよう配慮しました。

皆様の心の糧、そして知識の礎となるエッセイで全章を構成いたしましたので、きっとご満足いただけることと確信しております。

以下に挙げたねらいや目標を、頭にしっかり入れて学習すれば、学習効果が上がります。

1 Vocabulary Gallery

本文に出てくる語句の意味を確認しておくための練習問題です。これらの語句の意味をしっかりと確認して本文を読んでください。

2 Warm-up Dialogue

会話問題です。本文のテーマに関する日本人話者とネイティブスピーカーとの会話となっています。覚えておけば会話で使えるフレーズを中心に空欄にしていますので、音声を聞き、書き取ってください。また、実際に会話をしているつもりで練習をしてみましょう。チャプターのトピックについて英語で話す時の参考にしてください。

• Notes

会話文中に出てくる語句の解説です。会話文を読む際の参考にしてください。英文を読む時に役立つ文化情報なども入れています。

• Multiple Choice Questions

会話文について、その内容がどの程度理解できたかをチェックできます。

3 Ready to Read（本文）

250〜290語前後でまとめられた平易な名文です。Chapters 1-5 の平均語数が約260語、Chapters 6-10 の平均語数が約270語、Chapters 11-15 の平均語数が約280語になっており、段階的に少しずつ長い文を読んでいくことに慣れさせるようになっています。英文を読む楽しさを味わってください。音読もお勧めします。

• Notes

本文中に出てくる語句の解説です。英文を読む際の参考にしてください。英文を読む時に役立つ文化情報なども入れています。

• Comprehension Check-up

本文を読んだ直後に、その内容をどの程度理解できたかをチェックできます。

• Guided Summary

本文の内容が簡潔に要約されています。活用法をご自分で考えてみましょう。英文を要約する練習の解答例としても利用できます。

• Did You Know?

本文の内容に関連して、コラムを書いています。英語学習で疲れた頭を休めてもらいながら読んでもらえばいいですが、関連知識を提供し、さらに学習を進めてもらい、教養も高めてもらえるように内容を考えています。お楽しみに！

4 Language Highlights

各章の本文でフォーカスされている文法重要事項について、まとめて説明をしています。高校時代までに習ったはずの文法事項だと思いますが、再確認してみましょう。英文法は、英語を理解し使用するための基礎です。英文法の基礎がしっかりしていれば、その上に頑丈でしっかりした建物を建てることができるのです。

• Grammar Practice

日本語訳を参考に、与えられた語句を並べ替えて正しい英文を作る問題です。チャプターで習う文法事項に関連した問題ですので、Language Highlights の説明を参考に解いてみましょう。しっかりとできるまで何度でも挑戦してみましょう。全て正解できるようになったら、語群を隠して和文英訳問題としても挑戦してみてください。

5 Slash Reading Challenge

やや長い英文を、チャンク（単語の意味のあるまとまり）でとらえる練習をします。その後、音声で聞くリスニング、発話するスピーキング練習へとつながっていきます。

6 Let's Talk about It!

文字通り「それについて、話してみましょう！」 各章で述べられている健康トピックについて、あなたの考えを英語で述べる練習をする問題です。留学や仕事などで英語を使う場合、自分の意見をその理由ともに表現できることは極めて重要なことです。ペア練習などで他人の意見を聞く練習もしてください。

CONTENTS

Chapter 1

Sleep Is Important

1 Vocabulary Gallery   1-02

以下のイラストを参考にして、英文の下線部の意味を枠内の選択肢より選んで記号（a～f）で答えましょう。

| ① infant(s) | ② stress | ③ concentrate |
| gain weight | patient(s) | accident(s) |

1. <u>Infants</u> need more sleep than adults.   (   )
2. <u>Stress</u> is very bad for your health.   (   )
3. She's too tired to <u>concentrate</u> on her homework.   (   )
4. The boy <u>gains weight</u> when he's tired.   (   )
5. Dr. Takahashi always tells his <u>patients</u> to sleep seven hours.   (   )
6. Tired drivers cause many serious auto <u>accidents</u>.   (   )

| a) 体重が増加する | b) 患者 | c) 事故 |
| d) 集中する | e) 心理的負担 | f) 乳幼児 |

2 Warm-up Dialogue CD 1-03

交換留学生のカズトは友人のマギーと期末試験について話をしたいようです。音声を聞いて、空欄に聞き取った英語を書きましょう。

Kazuto: Hey, Maggie. I (   ) (   ) (   ) to you about the final exam.

Maggie: NOT NOW!! Can't you see I'm busy?

Kazuto: Wow! You're really in a bad mood! What's wrong?

Maggie: I can't (   ) (   ) my homework. I'm SO tired. That's why I'm in such a bad mood.

Kazuto: OK, Maggie. I get it, but you've gotta sleep more. With seven hours every night, you'll feel better and think better. Believe me!

Maggie: You're right. Last night I got only three hours of sleep. (   ) (   ) I'm such a mess.

Notes
That's why ～: だから～
be in a bad mood: 機嫌が悪い
you've gotta: ～しなきゃ、～しなけりゃ（you have to のくだけた形）
a mess: 取り乱した人

Multiple Choice Questions

空欄に入る最も適切なものを選びましょう。

1. Maggie doesn't want to speak with Kazuto because _____.
   a. she doesn't like him
   b. she's busy
   c. she's in a bad mood

2. Maggie is in a bad mood because _____.
   a. she doesn't like homework
   b. Kazuto is talking to her
   c. she's too tired to concentrate

3. Kazuto tells Maggie that she'll feel and think better if _____.
   a. she sleeps seven hours every night
   b. she's in a bad mood
   c. she sleeps three hours every night

3 Ready to Read 1-04

Do you sleep enough? Like many people, you probably don't. According to sleep specialists, the average adult should sleep seven to eight hours every night. Children,
5 especially infants, need more.

Sleep is important for your health. After a good night's sleep, you feel better because your body is rested and your mind is clear. You have more energy to solve problems, so you have less stress. You are healthier because sleep strengthens your immune system.

10 When you sleep enough, you look better, even younger. Your face is rested, and your eyes are clear. That's why American mothers often tell their daughters to go to bed and get their *beauty sleep.*

Sleep loss is bad for your health. When you are tired, you can't concentrate. You make more mistakes. You may even fall asleep in class or at
15 work.

Tired people have more health problems. They get sick more often. They are irritable, and frequently in a bad mood. When they are stressed, their blood pressure goes up. Many gain weight. Some even develop diabetes.

Sleep loss creates serious problems for society. Companies lose money
20 when employees take too many sick days. Doctors have to see more patients. More people have to be hospitalized.

There are also safety concerns. Tired workers, especially those using dangerous machines, get injured more often. Sleepy drivers cause many serious accidents on the roads and highways.

25 Now you understand why sleep is important. Please take my advice, and get seven hours of sleep. You'll feel better, look better, and think better.

(Words: 255)

be rested: 休まって	**diabetes:** 糖尿病
strengthen(s): 強化する	**sick days:** 病気休暇、病欠
immune system: 免疫系、免疫機構	

Notes

Comprehension Check-up

本文の内容に合っている文には T を、合っていない文には F を [　] に記入しましょう。

1. When you sleep enough, you have more energy and more stress. [　]
2. When people don't sleep enough, they make mistakes because they can't concentrate. [　]
3. Sleep loss can cause serious health problems such as high blood pressure, weight gain and even diabetes. [　]
4. It's not safe for people to drive or use dangerous machines when they are tired. [　]

Guided Summary 🎧 1-05

次の英文は本文を要約したものです。(1) から (8) の空所に、下の (a) ～ (h) から適語を選んで記入し文を完成させましょう。

Sleep is important for your health. (1)_____ need seven to eight hours every night. When you are rested, you feel better, think better, and look better. Sleep (2)_____ is bad for your health. You get sick more often, feel (3)_____, and may have higher blood pressure. Sleep loss (4)_____ many problems for (5)_____, doctors and hospitals. There are also (6)_____ concerns. Tired workers get (7)_____ more often. Sleepy drivers cause many (8)_____. So get enough sleep!

Word List

(a) companies	**(b)** irritable	**(c)** accidents	**(d)** safety
(e) adults	**(f)** injured	**(g)** creates	**(h)** loss

Did You Know?

私たちの個人体内時計は、私たちの睡眠覚醒サイクルをコントロールします。有名な睡眠についての専門家であるマイケル・ブレウス博士は、4 つの睡眠覚醒サイクルを描写するために動物の名前を使います。「イルカ」はよく寝られない人です。「ライオン」は朝はエネルギッシュですが、夜までには疲れてしまいます。「クマ」は多くの睡眠を必要とします。「オオカミ」は朝は疲れていますが、夜はエネルギッシュです。あなたはどのタイプですか？

4 Language Highlights

when の使い方

◇時を尋ねる when（疑問詞の when）

時を尋ねる疑問文では、疑問詞の when を使います。語順は直接疑問文では、when を文頭に置き、以降は疑問文の語順となり、間接疑問文では、when の後ろは平叙文の語順となります。

▶直接疑問文

When are you sleepy?（あなたはいつ眠いですか？）

▶間接疑問文

You have to know when you are sleepy.（あなたは自分がいつ眠いのかを知っておかなければなりません）

◇「～した（する）時に」を表す when（接続詞の when）

時を表す接続詞の代表格が when です。「～した（する）時に」などの意味を表します。

When you are tired, you can't concentrate.（本文第 4 段落）

◇時を説明する when（関係副詞の when）

関係副詞の when は、その時がどのような時かを説明する形容詞節を結びつける働きをします。この場合の関係副詞の when は on [at, in] which と置き換え可能です。

If you can't concentrate on your work, it is the time when you have to go to bed.
（もしあなたが仕事（勉強）に集中できないのなら、その時が就寝すべき時です）

Grammar Practice

次の日本語文に合うように英語文を完成させましょう。ただし文頭に来る語も小文字にしてあります。

1. あなたはいつ東京に行くつもりですか？

are/ when / Tokyo / you / to / to / going / go

_____

2. あなたが十分に睡眠をとる時には、あなたはとてもいい気分です。

you / you / when / very / enough, / good / sleep / feel

_____

3. あなたが夜帰宅しなければならない時には、気をつけなさい。

go / you / when / be / home / have to / at night, / careful

_____

4. 最初の東京オリンピックがいつ開催されたかあなたは知っていますか？

when / you / Tokyo Olympic Games / do / held / know / the first / were

_____

5. 郷に入れば郷に従え（諺）。

in / do / do / when / the / Rome, / as / Romans

_____

5 Slash Reading Challenge 🔊 1-06

日本文の意味のかたまりに従って、英文にスラッシュ（/）を入れましょう。次に音声を聞いて区切りごとに発話してみましょう。

1. 十分な睡眠を取った後は、／あなたは気分がよいです／なぜなら身体が休息し／そして心も晴れるから

   After a good night's sleep, you feel better because your body is rested and your mind is clear.

2. 眠気を感じているドライバーは引き起こします／多くの深刻な事故を／一般道や高速道路で

   Sleepy drivers cause many serious accidents on the roads and highways.

6 Let's Talk about It!

1. Tell your partners how you feel when you don't get enough sleep.

2. Discuss with your partners the problems that sleep loss creates for society and businesses.

Chapter 2
Is Salt Bad for Us?

1 Vocabulary Gallery 🎵 1-07

以下のイラストを参考にして、英文の下線部の意味を枠内の選択肢より選んで記号（a ～ f）
で答えましょう。

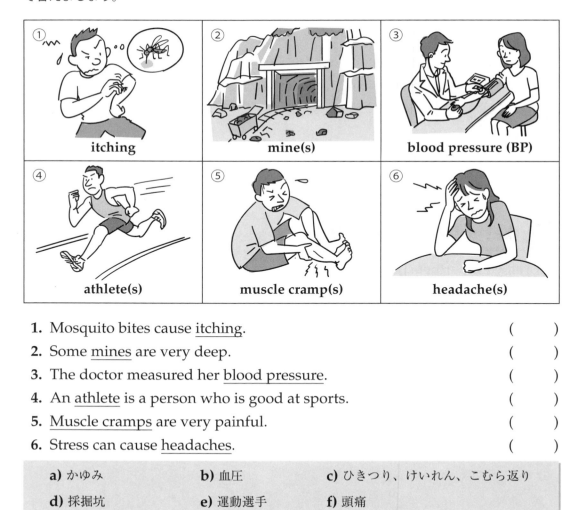

① itching	② mine(s)	③ blood pressure (BP)
④ athlete(s)	⑤ muscle cramp(s)	⑥ headache(s)

1. Mosquito bites cause <u>itching</u>. 　　　　　　　　　　　　　(　)
2. Some <u>mines</u> are very deep. 　　　　　　　　　　　　　　(　)
3. The doctor measured her <u>blood pressure</u>. 　　　　　　　(　)
4. An <u>athlete</u> is a person who is good at sports. 　　　　　(　)
5. <u>Muscle cramps</u> are very painful. 　　　　　　　　　　　(　)
6. Stress can cause <u>headaches</u>. 　　　　　　　　　　　　　(　)

a) かゆみ	**b)** 血圧	**c)** ひきつり、けいれん、こむら返り
d) 採掘坑	**e)** 運動選手	**f)** 頭痛

2 Warm-up Dialogue 🔊 1-08

サチコは交換留学生である友人のボビーが辛そうにしているのを心配しています。音声を聞いて、空欄に聞き取った英語を書きましょう。

Sachiko: (   ) (   ), Bobby?

Bobby: Ouh ouh (groaning in pain). I have a terrible muscle cramp in my leg. It HURTS so much.

Sachiko: You can get muscle cramps when you exercise and perspire too much. Your body doesn't have enough salt.

Bobby: But my doctor (   ) (   ) (   ) eat less salt because my BP is high. I don't want to have (   ) (   ) (   ).

Sachiko: He's right, but you've gotta remember that your body needs salt when you exercise and perspire.

Bobby: So salt isn't always bad for us. Interesting!

Notes
groan: うなる、うめく
perspire: 発汗する、汗をかく

Multiple Choice Questions

空欄に入る最も適切なものを選びましょう。

1. Bobby has a muscle cramp in his leg because _____.
   a. he uses too much salt
   b. he perspired a lot when he was exercising
   c. he has high blood pressure

2. Sachiko tells Bobby that _____.
   a. exercise is bad for his body
   b. eating too much salt causes muscle cramps
   c. too little salt in your body can cause muscle cramps

3. The doctor told Bobby to use less salt because _____.
   a. he had a heart attack
   b. he has high blood pressure
   c. he has to exercise more

3 Ready to Read 🔘 1-09

Salt is important. Humans need it, and so
do animals. With no salt or too little salt, our
bodies cannot function properly. Salt also has
many practical uses. It preserves food, reduces
5 swelling, stops itching, helps healing, calms a
sore throat, and even removes stains.

In the past, salt used to be very expensive – almost as much as gold! It
took a lot of time to collect salt from seawater (by evaporation) or from
underground mines. Thanks to modern technology, the production of salt has
10 increased, so the price has gone down.

Today many people worry about the health risks of salt. According to
medical research, eating too much salt can be dangerous. It raises blood
pressure, and thus increases the risk of a stroke or heart attack. For this reason,
many doctors and health professionals urge people to use less salt.

15 Sometimes salt is good for us. Athletes, dancers and people who work
outdoors perspire a lot, so their bodies need more salt. Salt deficiency – that is,
not enough salt in your body – can cause muscle cramps, headaches, dizziness,
weakness and, in extreme cases, even death.

Did you know that there are many different kinds of salt? Some are
20 healthier than others. Common table salt, for instance, is highly processed,
and contains additives. That's why you should use natural, unprocessed salt
such as sea salt or pink Himalayan salt. These natural salts cost more, but are
better for your body.

Is salt bad for us? Sometimes it is, but sometimes it isn't. It just depends
25 on *how much* we use and *what kind* we choose.

(Words: 266)

Notes		
preserve: 保存する	**deficiency:** 不足
swelling: 腫れ	**dizziness:** めまい、立ちくらみ
sore throat: のどの痛み	**weakness:** 虚弱
stain(s): しみ	**additive(s):** 添加物
evaporation: 蒸発	**Himalayan salt:** ヒマラヤ岩塩
health professional(s): 医療専門職者	

Comprehension Check-up

本文の内容に合っている文には T を、合っていない文には F を [　] に記入しましょう。

1. Our bodies need salt to function properly. [　　]
2. When you use less salt, the risk of a stroke or heart attack increases. [　　]
3. Salt deficiency can cause problems such as muscle cramps and headaches.

    [　　]
4. Table salt is good for your body because it's highly processed. [　　]

Guided Summary 🎧 1-10

次の英文は本文を要約したものです。(1) から (8) の空所に、下の (a) 〜 (h) から適語を選んで記入し文を完成させましょう。

Salt is important because our bodies need salt to (1)_____ properly.
According to medical (2)_____, eating too much salt, however, is (3)_____
because it raises blood pressure and (4)_____ the risk of a (5)_____ or
heart (6)_____. But athletes, dancers and people who work (7)_____
need more salt because they perspire more. Natural salts are (8)_____ for
your body than table salt. So salt is both good and bad for us.

Word List

(a) attack	**(b)** research	**(c)** dangerous	**(d)** increases
(e) outdoors	**(f)** better	**(g)** function	**(h)** stroke

Did You Know?

古代ローマ人はサラダが大好きだったことは皆さんご存じでしたか？ 「サラダ（salad）」という語は、ラテン語で「塩からい」を意味する salata に由来します。サラダのための野菜類はまず塩水に浸されました。この工程で味が加えられるとともに、防腐剤の機能も加えられました。古代ローマ人は塩が時には健康によくないことは、明らかに、知らなかったか、あるいは気にしなかったかのどちらかでしょう。

4 Language Highlights

◇現在形

be 動詞	am, is, are の3種類
一般動詞	原形と同じ形。3人称単数の場合は原形に (e)s をつける。

1．現在の「状態・習慣」などを表す

She is worried.（彼女は心配しています）

You feel better.（Chapter 1 第2段落）

2．「一般的な事実」を表す

Salt is important.（本文第1段落）

◇過去形

be 動詞	was, were の2種類
一般動詞	原形＋ed の形。ただし不規則変化も多い。

過去の時点における行動や状態や出来事などを表します。

It took a lot of time to collect salt from seawater.（本文第2段落）

◇現在完了形

「have [has] ＋過去分詞」という形で、「完了」「結果」「経験」「継続」などの意味を表します。過去の出来事が何らかの形で現在に影響を与えているというニュアンスを表します。

The production of salt has increased.（本文第2段落）

The price has gone down.（本文第2段落）

Grammar Practice

次の日本語文に合うように英語文を完成させましょう。ただし文頭に来る語も小文字にしてあります。

1. 十分に眠ることはあなたの健康にとってとても大切です。

enough / is / your / sleeping / health / important / very / for

_____

2. ピンク色のヒマラヤ岩塩は、普通のテーブル塩より健康的です。

Himalayan / common / salt / table salt / than / pink / healthier / is

_____

3. 海水から塩を集めることはとても時間がかかりました。

a lot of / collect / time / seawater / to / from / salt / took

_____

4. 過去には塩の値段はとても高かったです。

the past, / expensive / salt / in / very / of / the price / was

_____

5. 彼女は以前ヒマラヤ山脈に行ったことがあります。

has / before / Mountains / she / to / Himalaya / been / the

_____

5 Slash Reading Challenge 🎧 1-11

日本文の意味のかたまりに従って、英文にスラッシュ（ / ）を入れましょう。次に音声を聞いて区切りごとに発話してみましょう。

1. 全く塩がなく／あるいは塩が少なすぎると／私たちの身体は／適切に機能しません
   With no salt or too little salt, our bodies cannot function properly.

2. この理由のため／多くの医師たち／そして医療専門者たちは／人々に求めます／より少ない塩を使うことを
   For this reason, many doctors and health professionals urge people to use less salt.

6 Let's Talk about It!

1. Discuss with your partners some of the practical uses of salt.

2. Discuss with your partners the dangers of eating too much/too little salt.

Chapter 3

Water Is Wonderful

1 Vocabulary Gallery 🎧 1-12

以下のイラストを参考にして、英文の下線部の意味を枠内の選択肢より選んで記号（a 〜 f）で答えましょう。

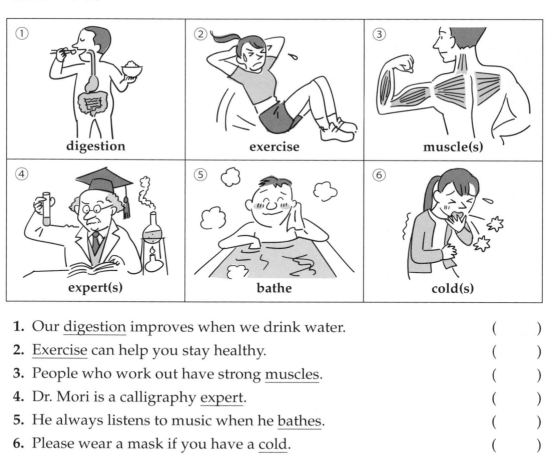

① digestion	② exercise	③ muscle(s)
④ expert(s)	⑤ bathe	⑥ cold(s)

1. Our <u>digestion</u> improves when we drink water. (　　)
2. <u>Exercise</u> can help you stay healthy. (　　)
3. People who work out have strong <u>muscles</u>. (　　)
4. Dr. Mori is a calligraphy <u>expert</u>. (　　)
5. He always listens to music when he <u>bathes</u>. (　　)
6. Please wear a mask if you have a <u>cold</u>. (　　)

a) 専門家	b) 風邪	c) 運動（する）
d) 消化	e) 筋肉	f) 入浴する

2 Warm-up Dialogue 🎧 1-13

ヨシと彼のアメリカ人の友人メリッサはジムで運動をしていましたが、突然、メリッサが痛みに叫び出してしまいました。音声を聞いて、空欄に聞き取った英語を書きましょう。

Melissa: Oww . . . ouch . . . oww. Yoshi, my leg hurts so much. I have a terrible muscle cramp. Oww!!

Yoshi: (　　　　　) (　　　　　　　), Melissa. You'll be OK. Now here drink some water because you're dehydrated. Is the pain (　　　　　) (　　　　　)?

Melissa: Yes. Thanks so much, Yoshi. I'm beginning to feel better. Wow, that cramp really hurt.

Yoshi: Listen, Melissa. (　　　　　) (　　　　　) drink more, especially when you exercise. You get muscle cramps when you're dehydrated.

Melissa: You're so right, Yoshi. Next time I exercise, I promise I'll drink more water.

> **Notes**
> **ouch:** 痛いっ（痛い時に口から出る言葉）
> **dehydrated:** 脱水状態の

Multiple Choice Questions

1、2 は空欄に入る最も適切なものを選びましょう。3 は適切な答えを選びましょう。

1. Melissa has a muscle cramp because _____.
   a. her leg hurts so much
   b. she is dehydrated
   c. she doesn't exercise often

2. Yoshi tells Melissa that the best way to stop muscle cramps is to _____.
   a. exercise more often
   b. stop exercising
   c. drink more water

3. Will Melissa follow Yoshi's advice?
   a. Yes.
   b. No.
   c. Maybe.

3 Ready to Read 🎵 1-14

Did you know that almost 60% of our body is water? That is why water plays a key role in making our body function properly. Now let's look at some of the reasons why
5 water is wonderful.

First of all, water stimulates digestion of the food we eat. It helps us eliminate liquid waste from our bladder and solid waste from our intestines. Water also produces the saliva and mucus, which keep our mouth, nose and eyes moist.

10 The wonders of water do not stop there. Water improves circulation, and also energizes our muscles. In addition to maintaining blood pressure, it also controls body temperature. Last but not least, it makes our skin look fresh and healthy.

Every day, our body loses water. If we don't replace the water we lose,
15 our body becomes dehydrated. Why is dehydration dangerous? It's because it causes muscle cramps, joint pain, dizziness and, in extreme cases, death. That's why it's very important to drink water.

How much water should we drink to replace the water we lose? Most experts suggest 4 - 6 glasses daily. Individuals who exercise a lot or who work
20 outdoors should drink more.

When we bathe, water cleans our body, and makes our skin fresh. Handwashing is particularly important because it removes germs. Medical experts remind people that this healthy habit reduces the risk of infection from the viruses, which can cause colds and flu.

25 If you want to stay healthy, please drink enough water, and wash your hands frequently. Don't you agree that water is wonderful?

(Words: 257)

Notes		
play(s) a key role: 重要な役割を演ずる	**mucus:** 粘液	
stimulate(s): 刺激する	**dizziness:** めまい	
eliminate: 排出する	**infection:** 感染症	
bladder: 膀胱	**flu:** インフルエンザ （influenza の短縮語）	
saliva: 唾液		

Comprehension Check-up

本文の内容に合っている文には T を、合っていない文には F を [   ] に記入しましょう。

1. Water is wonderful because it helps our body function properly.   [   ]

2. Dehydration happens when we don't replace the water our body loses.

   [   ]

3. Individuals who exercise a lot should drink 4 - 6 glasses of water daily.

   [   ]

4. Frequent handwashing reduces the risk of infection from germs and viruses.   [   ]

Guided Summary   🎧 1-15

次の英文は本文を要約したものです。(1) から (8) の空所に、下の (a) ～ (h) から適語を選んで記入し文を完成させましょう。

Water makes our body (1)_____ properly. It stimulates our (2)_____, improves (3)_____, (4)_____ our muscles, maintains blood pressure, controls body (5)_____, and makes our skin look healthy. We should drink 4 - 6 glasses of water to (6)_____ the water we lose daily – more if we (7)_____ a lot. Water cleans our body, and removes (8)_____ from our hands. Water is indeed wonderful.

Word List

| (a) circulation | (b) replace | (c) germs | (d) function |
| (e) energizes | (f) digestion | (g) exercise | (h) temperature |

Did You Know?

水を飲むと、あなたの傷が早く治ることはご存知でしたか？　水は傷口に酸素や他の栄養素をもたらすので、治癒のプロセスが加速するのです。もし歯ぐきから出血したら、この簡単な方法を試してみましょう。グラス一杯のぬるま湯に塩を少々加え、そしてうがいをしてみましょう。塩水は、炎症も抑え、感染も防ぎます。

4 Language Highlights

why の使い方

◇理由を尋ねる why（疑問詞の why）

疑問詞の why は「何のために、なぜ」であるのかを尋ねる疑問文で使われます。

Why is dehydration dangerous?（本文第 4 段落）

◇理由を修飾する why（関係副詞の why）

関係副詞の why は、何の理由であるのかを説明する場合に使われます。

There are many reasons (why) water is important.（水が大切な理由はたくさんあります）

関係副詞の why の先行詞は reasons となります。

That's why it's very important to drink water.（本文第 4 段落）

That's why ～で「それが～の理由である」という意味を表します。This is the reason why の先行詞 the reason が省略されたとも、why の中に先行詞が含まれるとも考えられます。

◇その他の why を用いた表現

その他、why を用いた重要表現に次のようなものがあります。

It's hot. Why don't you drink this cold water?（暑いねえ。この冷たい水を飲みなよ）

Why don't you ～? で「～しませんか、～した方がいいですよ」などの提案・忠告を表します。ここでは、「あなたが、この冷たい水を飲まないのはなぜなのか」と飲まない理由を尋ねているのではなく、「なぜ、飲まないということがあろうか、そんな理由はない、ぜひ飲んでください」という提案です。

Why, it's 35 ℃ outdoors!（あらまあ、外は（摂氏）35 度だよ！）

why は間投詞としても使われ、「おや、まあ」など驚き・不満などの気持ちを表します。

Grammar Practice

次の日本語文に合うように英語文を完成させましょう。ただし文頭に来る語も小文字にしてあります。

1. あなたはなぜ多くの水を飲まなくてはならないのですか？

   drink / do / why / to / water / you / a lot of / have

   _____

2. なぜ入学試験で英語が重要なのですか？

   English / why / entrance / is / important / the / in / examination

   _____

3. それが、この俳優が女の子たちに人気がある理由です。

   why / girls / this / that's / is / popular / actor / among

   _____

4. これが、私が毎日英語を勉強し続ける理由です。

   is / this / why / English / studying / every day / keep / I

   _____

5. おやまあ、また強い台風が日本に接近しているよ！

   typhoon / why / another / Japan / approaching / strong / again / is

   _____

5 Slash Reading Challenge 🔵 CD 1-16

日本文の意味のかたまりに従って、英文にスラッシュ（ / ）を入れましょう。次に音声を聞いて区切りごとに発話してみましょう。

1. 水は私たちが液体の老廃物を排出するのを助けます／私たちの膀胱から／そして固形の老廃物を／私たちの腸から

   Water helps us eliminate liquid waste from our bladder and solid waste from our intestines.

2. 最後に重要なことを述べますが／水は私たちの皮膚を／みずみずしくそして健康に見せます

   Last but not least, water makes our skin look fresh and healthy.

6 Let's Talk about It!

1. Discuss with your partners some of the reasons why water is wonderful.

2. Discuss with your partners why handwashing is an important and healthy habit.

Chapter 4

Hot Springs: A Miracle of Nature

1 Vocabulary Gallery 🎧 1-17

以下のイラストを参考にして、英文の下線部の意味を枠内の選択肢より選んで記号（a～f）で答えましょう。

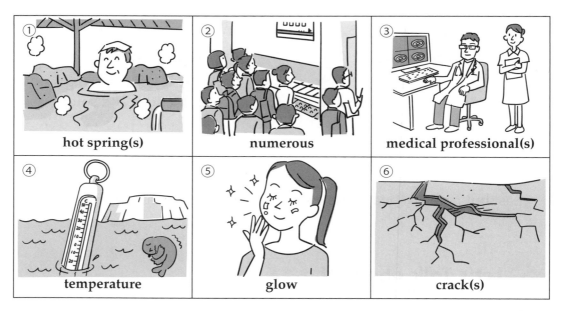

① hot spring(s)	② numerous	③ medical professional(s)
④ temperature	⑤ glow	⑥ crack(s)

1. Soaking in a <u>hot springs</u> is very relaxing.　　　　　　　（　　）
2. There are <u>numerous</u> people waiting for the subway.　　　（　　）
3. Doctors, nurses and physical therapists are <u>medical professionals</u>.　（　　）
4. The <u>temperature</u> of the ocean water at the North Pole is very cold.　（　　）
5. Junko's skin has a healthy <u>glow</u>.　　　　　　　　　　　　（　　）
6. An earthquake can create large <u>cracks</u> in the ground.　　（　　）

a) 多い、多くの	b) 温度	c) ひび、割れ目、裂け目
d) 医療専門職	e) 輝き	f) 温泉

2 Warm-up Dialogue 🎧 1-18

ラルフは友人のジュンコに週末の温泉旅行について尋ねています。音声を聞いて、空欄に聞き取った英語を書きましょう。

Ralph: Hi, Junko. You (　　　　　) (　　　　　)! You must have enjoyed visiting Beppu.

Junko: It was DIVINE! I mean, soaking in those hot springs (　　　　　) (　　　　　) for the body and the mind.

Ralph: So, did you go alone or with friends?

Junko: Going alone is no fun. I went with Satomi and two gals from Sendai.

Ralph: Sounds like (　　　　　) (　　　　　) (　　　　　). Can I come along next time you go there?

Junko: Sorry, Ralph, but the answer is NO. Our trips to the hot springs are for girls only.

Notes

divine: 素晴らしい
gal(s): 女子

Multiple Choice Questions

空欄に入る最も適切なものを選びましょう。

1. Junko had a great time in Beppu because _____.
   a. she went alone
   b. she looks fabulous
   c. soaking in the hot springs made her feel good

2. Junko went to Beppu _____.
   a. with Satomi and two other gals
   b. with two gals from Sendai
   c. alone

3. Ralph wants to go to Beppu with Junko, but she tells him _____.
   a. maybe next time
   b. yes, of course
   c. no because these trips are for girls only

3 Ready to Read 🎧 1-19

Do you know how hot springs are formed? Water from rain or melted snow goes deep inside the hot interior of the earth. There it is heated. Then it rises

5 through the cracks in the earth, and creates a hot spring.

The temperature of the water in hot springs varies. Sometimes it is so hot that it could burn you or even kill you. Other times, it's pleasantly warm. Soaking in such water relaxes your body and your mind.

10 You can find hot springs in countries all over the world. They are particularly numerous in active volcanic areas such as Japan, Peru, Italy, Iceland, Greenland, Turkey and the western parts of the USA.

Hot springs are not just a miracle of nature. Medical professionals recognize that they also do "miracles" for our health. The minerals in this

15 water help reduce pain from arthritis, rheumatism and sore muscles.

Soaking in this therapeutic water also detoxifies the body, and reduces stress. Less stress means lower blood pressure. After taking a bath in hot spring water, you see that your skin has a healthy glow.

Some hot springs have no entry fee, but if you feel weak or ill, there is

20 nobody to help. Other hot springs are surrounded by hotels, restaurants, shops and even parks. These are popular tourist destinations.

Today more and more people in other countries are discovering what the Japanese have known for centuries. Hot springs are good for your health – both physical and psychological.

25 That's why hot springs are indeed a miracle of nature.

(Words: 256)

Notes

burn: やけどさせる   **sore muscles:** 筋肉痛
arthritis: 関節炎   **entry fee:** 入場料
rheumatism: リウマチ

Comprehension Check-up

本文の内容に合っている文には T を、合っていない文には F を [　] に記入しましょう。

1. The water in hot springs is heated inside the earth's interior. [　]
2. The temperature of the water in hot springs is always the same. [　]
3. Hot springs with no entry fee can be dangerous because there is nobody to help if you feel weak or ill. [　]
4. Hot springs can help improve your physical and psychological health.

[　]

Guided Summary　🎧 1-20

次の英文は本文を要約したものです。(1) から (8) の空所に、下の (a) ～ (h) から適語を選んで記入し文を完成させましょう。

Hot springs are (1)_____ when water from rain or melted snow is (2)_____ inside the earth and rises to the surface. The (3)_____ of the water in hot springs varies. There are hot springs all over the world. Medical (4)_____ agree that soaking in hot springs does "miracles" for our health – physical and (5)_____. It reduces pain from arthritis and sore muscles, (6)_____ our body, and (7)_____ stress. Today more and more people are (8)_____ that hot springs are indeed a miracle of nature.

Word List

(a) psychological	(b) reduces	(c) detoxifies	(d) created
(e) temperature	(f) professionals	(g) discovering	(h) heated

Did You Know?

古代ローマ人は階級を問わず、入浴が好きであったことはご存知でしたか？　古代のローマ人たちは、特別な浴場に行き、そこで入浴をしながらリラックスをしたり、交流をしたり、仕事の交渉までもしたのです。ローマや他の都市の浴場はしばしば豪華な飾りつけのある手の込んだ建造物でした。そこには、常連客が読書をしたり、運動をしたり、美容施術を受けたりする特別な場所もあったのです。

4 Language Highlights

動名詞

動名詞を作るには動詞を〜 ing 形にします。動名詞の働きは次の４つです。

1.　主語

Soaking in such water relaxes your body and your mind.（本文第 2 段落）

Soaking (in such water) が文の主語になっています。

2.　be 動詞の補語

One of her hobbies is going to Japanese hot springs.（彼女の趣味の一つは、日本の温泉に行くことです）

going (to Japanese hot springs) が is の補語になっています。

3.　他動詞の目的語

You must have enjoyed visiting Beppu. (Warm-up Dialogue)

visiting (Beppu) は enjoyed の目的語になっています。なお、enjoy は不定詞を目的語にとらず動名詞を目的語にとります。

4.　前置詞の目的語

After taking a bath in hot spring water, you see that your skin has a healthy glow.
（本文第 5 段落）

taking (a bath in hot spring water) は前置詞 after の目的語になっています。

Grammar Practice

次の日本語文に合うように英語文を完成させましょう。ただし文頭に来る語も小文字にしてあります。

1. あなたはその地域のたくさんの温泉に入ってみて楽しみましたか？

   you / hot springs / in / have / trying / enjoyed / many / the area

   _____

2. 長時間風呂に浸かっていると、ふらふらすることがあります。

   makes / for / soaking in / a long time / dizzy / the bath / sometimes / you

   _____

3. あなたは帰宅した後、手をしっかり洗わなければなりません。

must / after / you / your hands / wash / thoroughly / home /coming

_____

4. 彼の新しい趣味は、友達とオンラインゲームをすることです。

is / new / his / his friends / hobby / with / playing / an online game

_____

5. 英語で映画を観ることは、リスニングを練習するいい方法です。

a good way / watching / English / films / practice listening / is / in / to

_____

5 Slash Reading Challenge 🎧 1-21

日本文の意味のかたまりに従って、英文にスラッシュ（ / ）を入れましょう。次に音声を聞いて区切りごとに発話してみましょう。

1. 時には／それはとても熱く／あなたをやけどさせ得ます／またはあなたを殺しさえもします

   Sometimes, it is so hot that it could burn you or even kill you.

2. この水の中のミネラルが／痛みを減らす助けになります／関節炎／リウマチ／そして筋肉痛からの

   The minerals in this water help reduce pain from arthritis, rheumatism and sore muscles.

6 Let's Talk about It!

1. Discuss with your partners why soaking in hot springs is good for your health.

2. Discuss with your partners why you like/don't like going to a Japanese *onsen*.

Chapter 5

Healthy Lessons from the Blue Zones

1 Vocabulary Gallery 🎧 1-22

以下のイラストを参考にして、英文の下線部の意味を枠内の選択肢より選んで記号（a 〜 f）で答えましょう。

| ① author(s) | ② legume(s) | ③ obesity |
| ④ household chores | ⑤ stairs | ⑥ social interaction(s) |

1. An <u>author</u> is a person who writes books. ( )
2. Peas, lentils, and beans are called <u>legumes</u>. ( )
3. An unhealthy diet can cause <u>obesity</u>. ( )
4. It takes time and energy to do all the <u>household chores</u>. ( )
5. Climbing <u>stairs</u> is good for your health. ( )
6. <u>Social interaction</u> makes people feel less lonely. ( )

a) 著者、筆者	**b)** 相互交流、社交	**c)** 階段
d) 豆類、マメ科	**e)** 肥満	**f)** 家事

2 Warm-up Dialogue 🎧 1-23

アツシはアメリカ人の友人ルシルに沖縄旅行について話しています。音声を聞いて、空欄に聞き取った英語を書きましょう。

Atsushi: Okinawa is like paradise – gorgeous beaches, friendly people and great food. You really should go.

Lucille: (　　　　　　) (　　　　　　　　　)? I'm going in March to do a research project about what Okinawans eat.

Atsushi: What?? That sounds SO boring. Why don't you just (　　　　　　) (　　　　　　　) on the beaches? That's more fun.

Lucille: Come on, Atsushi! Don't you know that Okinawans live longer than other people because of their healthy diet?

Atsushi: Hmmm . . . . So you'll be eating a lot. You'd better exercise, (　　　　　) (　　　　　　　) you'll get fat!

Lucille: Don't talk to me about getting fat! Yesterday you ate three huge hamburgers and fries. Now that's NOT a healthy diet.

> **Notes**
> **Okinawan(s):** 沖縄人、沖縄の住人
> **fries:** フライドポテト（French fries ともいう）

Multiple Choice Questions

空欄に入る最も適切なものを選びましょう。

1. Atsushi tells Lucille that she should visit Okinawa because _____.
   a. only the beaches are good
   b. Okinawans are not friendly
   c. it's like paradise

2. Lucille is going to Okinawa because _____.
   a. she wants to chill out on the beaches
   b. she wants to learn why Okinawans don't live long
   c. she wants to learn about the Okinawan diet

3. Lucille tells Atsushi that he will get fat if _____.
   a. he goes to the beach
   b. he eats too much fast food
   c. he eats healthy food

3 Ready to Read 🎧 1-24

Dan Buettner, author and journalist, traveled all over the world, and found five places where people live long, healthy lives. He drew a blue circle around them on his
5 map. That's why they are called Blue Zones.

The first is Okinawa. The Italian island of Sardinia is second, and a religious community in California is third. The Greek island of Icaria comes in fourth, while the Nicoya Peninsula in Costa Rica is fifth.

Buettner studied the lifestyle in the Blue Zones. He wanted to understand
10 why people there lived such long, healthy and happy lives. Here is what he learned.

First, people in the Blue Zones have a healthy diet – lots of vegetables, fruit, legumes, nuts and whole grains. They eat fish but very little meat. Often they drink wine with their meals. Because of their healthy diet, there are fewer
15 cases of heart disease, obesity and diabetes.

Second, people in these areas are physically active. During the day, they walk a lot, climb stairs, work in the garden, and do household chores. At night, they get enough sleep. Exercise and sleep promote good health.

Third, there is more social interaction in these communities than in urban
20 areas. People feel less lonely because neighbors know and help each other. Families live close by, so children can spend time with their grandparents and relatives.

Fourth, older people play an active role in their community. The younger generations respect the wisdom of their elders. This positive attitude toward
25 age keeps people "young at heart."

Don't you agree that these healthy lessons from the Blue Zones are important?

(Words: 266)

Notes

Sardinia: サルジニア島（イタリア西方の 地中海にある島）
religious community: 宗教的共同体
Icaria: ギリシャ北エーゲの島

Nicoya Peninsula: 太平洋に面するコスタリカの半島
whole grain(s): 全粒粉（穀物などの胚芽を除いていないもの）

本文の内容に合っている文には T を、合っていない文には F を [　] に記入しましょう。

1. Dan Buettner wanted to learn why people in the so-called Blue Zones live long, healthy lives. [　]

2. People in the Blue Zones have a healthy diet because they eat lots of vegetables, fruit, meat and nuts. [　]

3. People in the Blue Zones are physically active, but don't get enough sleep. [　]

4. In the Blue Zones, there is more social interaction among people of different ages. [　]

Guided Summary 🎧 1-25

次の英文は本文を要約したものです。(1) から (8) の空所に、下の (a) ～ (h) から適語を選んで記入し文を完成させましょう。

Dan Buettner found five places where people live long, (1)_____ lives. He wanted to (2)_____ why. In these so-called Blue Zones, people have a healthy (3)_____ with lots of vegetables, fruit, legumes, nuts and whole grains. They eat fish but little meat. In Blue Zone (4)_____, there is more social (5)_____ among (6)_____ and families. People help each other. Older people are active in the community. The younger (7)_____ respect their elders' (8)_____. These healthy lessons are important.

Word List

(a) diet	(b) generations	(c) healthy	(d) interaction
(e) wisdom	(f) communities	(g) understand	(h) neighbors

Did You Know?

多くの先進国で 3 世代以上の家族が増えていることはご存知でしたか？　一人暮らしをする金銭的余裕がない若い大人は、家から独立しません。3 世代が同居すると、働いている親は保育にお金をかける必要がありません。なぜならば祖父母が面倒を見てくれるからです。最近の調査では、祖父母と時間を過ごす子どもたちは、行動的および情緒的な問題を起こすことが少ないという指摘もあります。

4 Language Highlights

前置詞

名詞や代名詞などの前に置き、他の語との関係を表す語が前置詞です。以下に代表的な前置詞とその意味・用例を示します。

about（〜について、〜に関する）

<u>about</u> what Okinawans eat, <u>about</u> getting fat (Warm-up Dialogue)

around（〜の周りに、〜の周りを）

<u>around</u> them（本文第 1 段落）

at（〜を［に］〈地点・時点などを表す〉）

<u>at</u> night（本文第 5 段落）, look <u>at</u> some of the reasons（Chapter 3 本文第 1 段落）

in（〜の中に）

<u>in</u> California, <u>in</u> Costa Rica（本文第 2 段落）, <u>in</u> these areas, <u>in</u> the garden（本文第 5 段落）

of（〜の）

the Italian island <u>of</u> Sardinia, the Greek island <u>of</u> Icaria（本文第 2 段落）, cases <u>of</u> heart disease（本文第 4 段落）

on（〜の上に［で］、〜にたよって、〜について）

<u>on</u> his map（本文第 1 段落）, depend <u>on</u> 〜（Chapter 2 本文第 6 段落）,

a book <u>on</u> healthy diet（健康的な食事についての本）

to（〜に）

goes <u>to</u> the beach (Warm-up Dialogue Multiple Choice Questions 3)

toward（〜に対する、〜に向けて）

attitude <u>toward(s)</u> age（本文第 7 段落）, <u>toward(s)</u> the dream（夢に向かって）

with（〜と 、〜に関して）

<u>with</u> their grandparents（本文第 6 段落）, angry <u>with</u> him（彼のことを怒っている）

Grammar Practice

次の日本語文に合うように英語文を完成させましょう。ただし文頭に来る語も小文字にしてあります。

1. 彼はわからない単語の周りに赤い丸をつけました。

   a red circle / he / he / drew / around / about / the words / wasn't sure

2. 私はアリゾナのアメリカ原住民コミュニティに行きました。

Native Americans / went / a community / I / in / to / of / Arizona

_____

3. 私の友人は毎日食事とともにビールを飲んでいます。

beer / every day / mine / of / with / friends / drink / their meals

_____

4. よい温泉のために別府は日本人以外にもよく知られています。

because / is well-known / Beppu / its / of / to / good hot springs, / non-Japanese

_____

5. たとえその水泳選手は病床にいたとしても、彼女は人生に対してポジティブな姿勢を持っています。

toward / the swimmer / she has / even if / is sick / in bed, / a positive attitude / life

_____

5 Slash Reading Challenge 🎵 1-26

日本文の意味のかたまりに従って、英文にスラッシュ（ / ）を入れましょう。次に音声を聞いて区切りごとに発話してみましょう。

1. 第三に／より社会的交流があります／これらの地域には／都市の地域よりも

Third, there is more social interaction in these communities than in urban areas.

2. この肯定的な態度が／年齢に対する／人々を保ちます／「心を若く」

This positive attitude toward age keeps people "young at heart."

6 Let's Talk about It!

1. Discuss with your partners some of the reasons why people in the Blue Zones live longer than people in urban areas.

2. Discuss with your partners why you want/don't want to live in a big city.

Chapter 6 — *Unhealthy Habits*

1 Vocabulary Gallery 🎵 1-27

以下のイラストを参考にして、英文の下線部の意味を枠内の選択肢より選んで記号（a 〜 f）
で答えましょう。

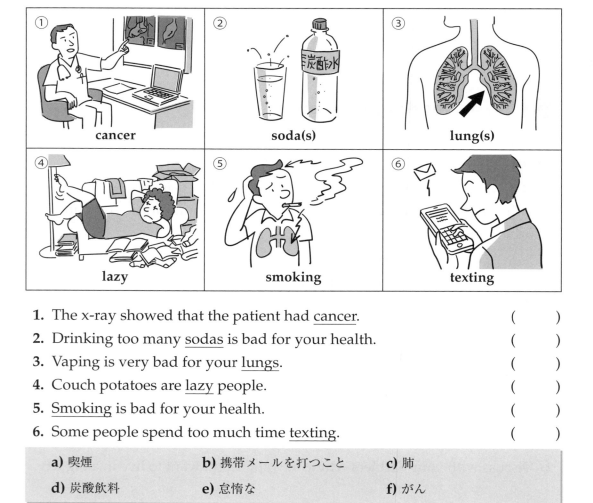

① cancer	② soda(s)	③ lung(s)
④ lazy	⑤ smoking	⑥ texting

1. The x-ray showed that the patient had <u>cancer</u>.   (   )
2. Drinking too many <u>sodas</u> is bad for your health.   (   )
3. Vaping is very bad for your <u>lungs</u>.   (   )
4. Couch potatoes are <u>lazy</u> people.   (   )
5. <u>Smoking</u> is bad for your health.   (   )
6. Some people spend too much time <u>texting</u>.   (   )

a) 喫煙	b) 携帯メールを打つこと	c) 肺
d) 炭酸飲料	e) 怠惰な	f) がん

2 Warm-up Dialogue CD 1-28

アメリカ人交換留学生のスティーブは、友人のチヅルに自分の不健康な習慣について話しています。音声を聞いて、空欄に聞き取った英語を書きましょう。

Steve: Oh, Chizuru. I'm really worried. I think I'm becoming a couch potato.

Chizuru: What's a couch potato? That's a new expression for me.

Steve: Well, it's somebody who sits on a couch, watches too much TV, and (   ) (   ) too much junk food.

Chizuru: Steve, those are really unhealthy habits. You're going to (   ) (   ).

Steve: (   ) (   ) (   ) (   )! I'm beginning to look like a potato.

Chizuru: Now listen to me, Steve. Stop being a couch potato. You've gotta start eating healthy and exercising. OK?

> **Note** expression: 表現

(**Multiple Choice Questions**)

空欄に入る最も適切なものを選びましょう。

1. A couch potato is a person who _____.
   a. eats too many potatoes
   b. watches too much TV and snacks on junk food
   c. doesn't eat too much junk food

2. Chizuru is worried because Steve _____.
   a. used to be fat
   b. never eats too much junk food
   c. has unhealthy habits

3. Chizuru tells Steve that he must _____.
   a. exercise so he can eat more junk food
   b. exercise and eat healthy
   c. watch more TV

In the previous chapters, we have read about how to live a healthy life. Now it's time to look at some unhealthy habits that are causing serious health problems.

5   Let's start with overeating. When people eat too much, especially if the food is unhealthy, they can gain weight. In the US and some developed nations, obesity is skyrocketing, even among children. These individuals tend to be at greater risk for heart disease, stroke or diabetes.

10   That's why it's important to eat healthy. Avoid fast food, fried food and sodas. To avoid overeating, eat slowly, and stop when you are about 80% full.

Smoking is an unhealthy habit, which weakens the lungs and, in many cases, causes lung cancer. E-cigarettes can help reduce nicotine craving. Unfortunately inhaling the vapor from e-cigarettes – *vaping*, as it is called – can
15 damage the lungs.

Today vaping is popular, particularly among teens and young adults. Many do not know that e-cigarettes contain nicotine as well as other chemicals, some of which can be very dangerous.

Are you a *couch potato*? This expression refers to a lazy individual who
20 watches too much TV and snacks on too much junk food. Couch potatoes gain weight because they don't exercise.

Today the number of couch potatoes is increasing because more and more people spend too much time texting, tweeting, playing video games and watching TV. As a result, they have no time or energy to work out, jog, do
25 yoga or take a walk.

The "cure" for these unhealthy habits is simple: eat less, don't smoke or vape, and exercise.

(Words: 261)

Notes
developed nations: 先進国	**chemicals:** 化学物質
e-cigarettes: 電子タバコ	

Comprehension Check-up

本文の内容に合っている文には T を、合っていない文には F を [　] に記入しましょう。

1. Obesity in developed nations is skyrocketing, but not among children.

   [　　]

2. Vaping is a safe, healthy way to stop smoking.　　　　　　　　[　　]

3. Couch potatoes have an unhealthy lifestyle because they vape too much on the couch.　　　　　　　　　　　　　　　　　　　　　　　　　　[　　]

4. If you eat less, don't smoke or vape, and exercise, you will have a healthier life.　　　　　　　　　　　　　　　　　　　　　　　　　　　　[　　]

Guided Summary　　🔵 1-30

次の英文は本文を要約したものです。(1) から (8) の空所に、下の (a) ～ (h) から適語を選んで記入し文を完成させましょう。

Unhealthy habits cause health problems. In the US and some developed nations, (1)＿＿＿＿ is (2)＿＿＿＿. These individuals are at greater (3)＿＿＿＿ for heart disease, stroke or diabetes. Smoking is unhealthy because it can cause (4)＿＿＿＿ cancer. E-cigarettes can help reduce (5)＿＿＿＿ craving, but they are bad for the lungs. Couch potatoes don't (6)＿＿＿＿ enough because they watch too much TV and (7)＿＿＿＿ on too much junk food. If you want to be healthy, eat less, don't smoke or (8)＿＿＿＿, and exercise.

Word List

(a) skyrocketing	(b) vape	(c) exercise	(d) obesity
(e) snack	(f) lung	(g) risk	(h) nicotine

● Did You Know? ●

たくさんの薬を飲み合わせること（多剤投与と呼びます）が危険であり得ることをご存知でしたか？　時に、これらの薬剤（処方薬、市販薬、健康サプリ類など）の相互作用が、予期しない有害な副作用を生み出します。だから、患者、特に高齢の患者は、医師に自分が服用している全ての薬剤のリストを示す必要があるのです。

4 Language Highlights

不定詞

「to ＋動詞の原形」の形を不定詞と呼び、次のような用法があります。

◇名詞用法

「～すること」と訳され、不定詞が文の主語、目的語、補語になります。

To eat healthy is important.（本文第 3 段落の文を改変）

◇形容詞用法

「～すべき」「～するための」の名詞を修飾する用法です。

It's time to look at some unhealthy habits.（本文第 1 段落）

They have no time or energy to work out.（本文第 7 段落）

◇副詞用法

「～するために」「～して」と動詞や形容詞等を修飾する方法です。

To avoid overeating, eat slowly, and stop when you are about 80% full.
（本文第 3 段落）

Grammar Practice

次の日本語文に合うように英語文を完成させましょう。ただし文頭に来る語も小文字にしてあります。

1. あなたが家にいなければならない時は、太りやすいです。

it's / when / to / have to / easy / stay home / you / get fat

_____

2. さあ、今が外出して楽しむ時です。

time / it's / and / now / go / to / out / have fun

_____

3. 私は、昨晩、目を覚ましているために一杯のコーヒーを飲みました。

to / I / a cup of / stay / last night / awake / drank / coffee

_____

4. 私たちは蕎麦の作り方を学びました。

how / have / soba / we / make / noodles / learned / to

_____

5. 温泉に行くことは、あなた自身をリラックスさせるためのよい方法です。

a good way / is / going / yourself / to / to / a hot spring / relax

_____

5 Slash Reading Challenge 🎵 1-31

日本文の意味のかたまりに従って、英文にスラッシュ（ / ）を入れましょう。次に音声を聞いて区切りごとに発話してみましょう。

1. 今／時間です／いくつかの不健康な習慣を見る／原因となる／重大な健康問題の

   Now it's time to look at some unhealthy habits that are causing serious health problems.

2. 多くの人は知りません／電子タバコがニコチンを含むことを／他の化学物質と同様に／そのうちのいくつかは／とても危険となり得るのです

   Many do not know that e-cigarettes contain nicotine as well as other chemicals, some of which can be very dangerous.

6 Let's Talk about It!

1. Discuss with your partners some healthy ways to avoid gaining weight.

2. Discuss with your partners why the number of couch potatoes is increasing.

Let's Dance!

1 Vocabulary Gallery 🎧 1-32

以下のイラストを参考にして、英文の下線部の意味を枠内の選択肢より選んで記号（a ～ f）で答えましょう。

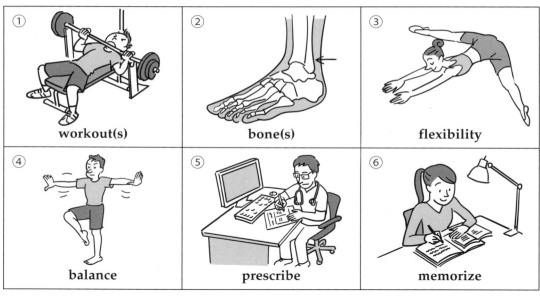

① workout(s)	② bone(s)	③ flexibility
④ balance	⑤ prescribe	⑥ memorize

1. His son really enjoys gym <u>workouts</u>. (　　)
2. When she fell, she broke one of the <u>bones</u> in her ankle. (　　)
3. Your <u>flexibility</u> increases when you dance. (　　)
4. With dance, your <u>balance</u> improves. (　　)
5. Doctors often <u>prescribe</u> dance therapy for older adults. (　　)
6. She has to <u>memorize</u> 100 new words for the TOEIC test. (　　)

a) 処方する	**b)** 骨	**c)** 均衡、つり合い
d) トレーニング、運動	**e)** 暗記する、覚える	**f)** 柔軟性

2 Warm-up Dialogue 🎧 1-33

アメリカに住む交換留学生のキヨシは、クラスメイトのジョアニーと運動について話しています。音声を聞いて、空欄に聞き取った英語を書きましょう。

Kiyoshi: OHH! Those online classes are SO long. Now I need to exercise. Hey, Joanie, (   ) (   ) (   ) with me?

Joanie: (   ) (   ), Kiyoshi! I really dislike jogging and all those sports-related activities.

Kiyoshi: You mean – you don't exercise? How can you stay fit?

Joanie: I dance! It's good for my body and my mind. When I dance, I feel really happy.

Kiyoshi: Well, when I jog, I just feel tired!

Joanie: So why don't you (   ) (   ) (   ) me to a salsa class? It's lots of fun, and the music is great.

> **Note**
> **salsa:** サルサ（速いテンポと複雑なリズムを特徴とするラテン音楽）

Multiple Choice Questions

空欄に入る最も適切なものを選びましょう。

1. Joanie doesn't go jogging with Kiyoshi because _____.
   - **a.** she really dislikes him
   - **b.** she is taking online classes
   - **c.** she really dislikes sports

2. Joanie likes dance because _____.
   - **a.** it's good only for the body
   - **b.** it's easier than sports
   - **c.** it's good for the mind and the body

3. When Kiyoshi jogs, he feels _____.
   - **a.** really happy
   - **b.** really tired
   - **c.** really unhappy

3 Ready to Read 🎧 1-34

Exercise, as we all know, helps us have a healthier life. Some people, however, don't like gym workouts, jogging, swimming or other sports-related activities. So how can we
5 stay fit? Let's dance!

Medical experts agree that dance is good for your body. In addition to building up muscles, it strengthens your bones, and thus reduces your risk of osteoporosis. With dance, your balance improves, and your flexibility increases.

10 When you dance, your heart beats faster, and pumps more oxygen to your lungs. A faster heartbeat helps lower your blood pressure. Lower blood pressure means that you have a lower risk of heart disease.

Dance is also good for your mind. First you memorize the body movements you will use. Next you listen to the rhythm of the music. When
15 you dance with the music, you can express your emotions. Then you'll feel happy.

One of the advantages of dance is its variety. You can choose a sexy tango, a lively salsa or an energetic zumba session. You can decide if you want to dance alone, with a partner or even in a group.

20 Today medical professionals often prescribe dance therapy for patients with degenerative diseases such as Parkinson's (PD) or Multiple Sclerosis (MS). Dancing, especially with a partner, improves balance, mobility and posture. Patients who dance tend to feel less stressed.

Dance is also a useful therapy for older adults, particularly those with
25 dementia. Dancing to music encourages them to move. It also helps reduce anxiety and, in some cases, even improves memory.

Now you understand why dance is a fun and healthy way to stay fit. So let's dance!

(Words: 270)

Notes

osteoporosis: 骨粗鬆症
tango: タンゴ（独特のリズムを持つラテン音楽またはラテン系社交ダンスの一種）
zumba: ズンバ（ラテン音楽を中心に行われるダンス・フィットネス）
degenerative disease(s):
　変性疾患（細胞や組織に変性が起こる疾患）

Parkinson's (PD):
　パーキンソン病（動作や歩行の困難や手の震えなど運動障害を示す進行性の神経変性疾患）
　(=Parkinson's disease)
Multiple Sclerosis (MS): 多発性硬化症
dementia: 認知症

Comprehension Check-up

本文の内容に合っている文にはTを、合っていない文にはFを［　　］に記入しましょう。

1. Medical experts believe that both sports and dance are healthy forms of exercise. ［　　］

2. You have a lower risk of heart disease when you have a slower heartbeat. ［　　］

3. In dance, your body movements follow the rhythm of the music. ［　　］

4. Dance therapy helps reduce stress in older adults and also people with degenerative diseases. ［　　］

Guided Summary 🎵 1-35

次の英文は本文を要約したものです。(1) から (8) の空所に、下の (a) ～ (h) から適語を選んで記入し文を完成させましょう。

If you dislike sports, dance is a healthy way to stay fit. It's good for your body because it (1)_____ muscles and bones. It also (2)_____ balance, increases flexibility, and lowers blood (3)_____. Dance is also good for your mind. First you must (4)_____ the body movements, and then listen to the (5)_____ of the music. When you dance with the music, you feel happy because you are expressing your (6)_____. Dance therapy helps (7)_____ stress among older adults and patients with degenerative (8)_____. So let's dance for health!

Word List

(a) pressure	(b) reduce	(c) strengthens	(d) emotions
(e) diseases	(f) memorize	(g) improves	(h) rhythm

Did You Know?

プロのダンサーとプロのスポーツ選手の人生には、多くの共通点があることを皆さんはご存知でしたか？　ダンスもスポーツも身体に負担を与えるので、けが（時にはキャリアを終わらせるようなけが）のリスクが高くなります。さらに、どちらの職業も競争が激しく、ストレスがかかります。だから、ほとんどのダンサーやプロスポーツ選手が 30 代半ばで引退するのは不思議ではありません。

④ Language Highlights

比較級

2つのものを比較し、等しくない場合は形容詞または副詞の比較級、あるいは「more/less ＋形容詞・副詞の原級」の形で表します。比較級の作り方は以下の通りです。

①一音節の形容詞・副詞の場合は、語尾に er をつけます。ただし e で終わる語は r だけをつけます。また y で終わる語は y を i に変えて er をつけます。

② more を使うのは、形容詞が二音節の語の一部、三音節以上の時です。

③不規則変化をする場合もあります。

When you dance, your heart beats <u>faster</u>.（本文第3段落）
Exercise helps us have a <u>healthier</u> life.（本文第1段落）
His cake is <u>more delicious</u> than mine.（彼のケーキは私のよりもおいしい）
I hope you will get <u>better</u> soon.（あなたが早くよくなることを願います）

④あるものが別のものより程度が低いことを示す劣等比較は「less ＋形容詞（副詞）の原級」の形を使います。

Patients who dance tend to feel <u>less stressed</u>.（本文第6段落）

⑤ little の比較級としての less や、many や much の比較級としての more もあります。

When you dance, your heart pumps <u>more</u> oxygen to your lungs.（本文第3段落）

Grammar Practice

次の日本語文に合うように英語文を完成させましょう。ただし文頭に来る語も小文字にしてあります。

1. 子どもたちが外で遊ぶ時、彼らは身体的により強くなります。

   children / when / outdoors, / physically / play / become / they / stronger

   _____

2. 皆、マリコは彼女の姉（妹）より美しいと思っています。

   Mariko / more / everybody thinks / is / that / her sister / than / beautiful

   _____

3. このような暑い日には、あなたはもっと水を飲む必要がありますよ。

like this / you / a hot day / drink / need to / more / on / water

_____

4. 私の新車はあなたのものより高価ではありません。

is / my / yours / less / than / car / new / expensive

_____

5. もしあなたが毎日練習したら、あなたはよりよい選手になるでしょう。

practice / if / you / you / better player / every day, / will be / a

_____

5 Slash Reading Challenge 🎧CD 1-36

日本文の意味のかたまりに従って、英文にスラッシュ（ / ）を入れましょう。次に音声を聞いて区切りごとに発話してみましょう。

1. より低い血圧は意味します／あなたがより低いリスクを持つこと／心臓疾患の

   Lower blood pressure means that you have a lower risk of heart disease.

2. 今日／医療専門職はしばしばダンス療法を処方します／変性疾患を持つ患者のために／パーキンソン病のような／あるいは多発性硬化症のような

   Today medical professionals often prescribe dance therapy for patients with degenerative diseases such as Parkinson's or Multiple Sclerosis.

6 Let's Talk about It!

1. Discuss with your partners why dance is good for both your body and your mind.

2. Discuss with your partners the reasons why you prefer/don't prefer dance over sports.

Chapter 8

The Story of Sugar

1 Vocabulary Gallery 🎧 1-37

以下のイラストを参考にして、英文の下線部の意味を枠内の選択肢より選んで記号（a 〜 f）で答えましょう。

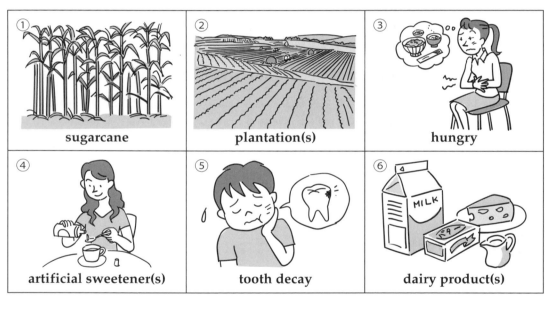

①	②	③
sugarcane	plantation(s)	hungry
④	⑤	⑥
artificial sweetener(s)	tooth decay	dairy product(s)

1. The <u>sugarcane</u> plant is two to four meters tall. (   )
2. There used to be many sugar <u>plantations</u> on the Caribbean islands. (   )
3. She was very <u>hungry</u> because she didn't have any lunch. (   )
4. She uses <u>artificial sweeteners</u> in her coffee rather than sugar. (   )
5. <u>Tooth decay</u> is painful and bad for your health. (   )
6. Milk, cream, butter and cheese are <u>dairy products</u>. (   )

a) 人工甘味料	b) 乳製品	c) 大農園、大農場
d) 空腹の、お腹がすいた	e) サトウキビ	f) 虫歯

2 Warm-up Dialogue CD 1-38

栄養学を専攻するトモコはクラスメイトのロジャーの食生活を心配しているようです。音声を聞いて、空欄に聞き取った英語を書きましょう。

Roger: Tomoko, I'm really depressed because I've gained so much weight in the (　　　　　) (　　　　　) (　　　　　). What should I do?

Tomoko: First of all, you have to eat less. Also you have to eat healthy food. So tell me what you've eaten today.

Roger: Not that much. I've had only three sodas, a bowl of cereal and two slices of chocolate cake. What's wrong with that?

Tomoko: (　　　　　) (　　　　　), Roger! All the food you're eating is full of added sugar. It's so unhealthy. No wonder you're gaining weight!

Roger: OK, Tomoko. Since you're the nutrition specialist, tell me what I should eat instead.

Tomoko: No more foods with added sugar like soda, cereal, cake and processed food. More foods with natural sugar like fruit, vegetables, (　　　　　) (　　　　　) and dairy products. Then you'll lose all that weight!

> **Notes**
> **not that much:** そんなにたくさんではないよ（この that は「そんなに」という意味の副詞）
> **nutrition:** 栄養学

Multiple Choice Questions

空欄に入る最も適切なものを選びましょう。

1. Roger is depressed because ＿＿＿＿＿＿.
   a. he needs to gain weight
   b. he is not eating enough
   c. he has gained weight

2. Tomoko tells Roger that ＿＿＿＿＿＿.
   a. some of the food he's eating has added sugar
   b. all of the food he's eating has added sugar
   c. all of the food he's eating needs added sugar

3. Tomoko tells Roger that he should eat ＿＿＿＿＿＿.
   a. more foods with natural sugar
   b. more foods with added sugar
   c. more foods like cereal and fruit

3 Ready to Read 🎵 1-39

Once upon a time, sugar was a luxury product that only the rich could afford. Today the consumption of sugar has skyrocketed because it is inexpensive and
5 plentiful. Now let's see how this increased use of sugar affects our health.

The sugarcane plant grows in hot, humid areas with lots of rain. Indigenous to Polynesia, sugar was later cultivated in Southern Asia and India. At first, the availability of sugar was limited. After the Europeans built huge
10 sugar plantations on the Caribbean islands, production increased, and the price dropped. Sugar was affordable.

The production of cane sugar no longer meets the demand. Now there are alternatives such as beet sugar, Stevia, corn syrup and artificial sweeteners. These sugars are added to many popular foods and drinks – sodas, fruit juices,
15 candy, cakes, cereals and processed foods.

Foods and drinks with *added sugar* are unhealthy. Since this sugar is digested rapidly, we feel hungry, overeat, and gain weight. Rapid digestion also causes a quick, sometimes dangerous, spike in blood sugar levels.

The healthy alternative to added sugar is the *natural sugar* in fruit,
20 vegetables, whole grains and dairy products. Natural sugar is digested slowly. As a result, we feel less hungry, and eat less. With slow digestion, our blood sugar levels do not spike.

The health consequences of consuming too much added sugar are alarming. Obesity is perhaps the most serious because it increases the risk of
25 heart disease. Obese individuals are also more likely to develop diabetes. People who consume too much sugar have more tooth decay.

If you want to be healthy, don't eat too much sugar!

(Words: 267)

Notes

once upon a time: 昔々	**Stevia:** ステビア（アマハステビアの葉から得られる
luxury product: ぜいたく品	低カロリーの甘味料）
the rich: お金持ち層	**corn syrup:** トウモロコシから作るシロップ
indigenous to 〜：〜の原産で	**spike:** 急上昇（する）

Comprehension Check-up

本文の内容に合っている文には T を、合っていない文には F を [　] に記入しましょう。

1. Today more people are eating sugar because it's inexpensive and plentiful.

   [　　]

2. Foods with added sugar are unhealthy because they are digested slowly.

   [　　]

3. It's better to have cereal and fruit juice rather than apples and milk. [　　]

4. Eating too much sugar causes health problems such as obesity, heart disease, diabetes and tooth decay.

   [　　]

Guided Summary 🎵 CD 1-40

次の英文は本文を要約したものです。(1) から (8) の空所に、下の (a) 〜 (h) から適語を選んで記入し文を完成させましょう。

Sugar was once a (1)_____ product, but now it is plentiful and (2)_____. Today cane sugar and other (3)_____ are added to many popular foods and drinks. They are unhealthy because added sugar is (4)_____ rapidly. Then we overeat, gain (5)_____, and have high blood pressure. Foods and drinks with (6)_____ sugar are a healthy alternative. Natural sugar is digested slowly, so we don't overeat or have blood pressure problems. Consuming too much sugar causes serious health problems such as (7)_____, heart disease, diabetes and tooth (8)_____.

Word List

(a) weight	(b) alternatives	(c) luxury	(d) obesity
(e) digested	(f) decay	(g) inexpensive	(h) natural

● Did You Know? ●

砂糖は身体にとって完璧な皮膚摩擦材であることは皆さんはご存知でしたか？ 「シュガースクラブ」といいますが、砂糖の中の小さく荒い粒子が死んだ細胞を剥ぎ落とし、あなたの皮膚をすべすべにしてくれるのです。 かかとやひじやひざのような、乾燥して荒れた部分には特に効果的です。 もし、ドライスキンや敏感肌の場合は、顔にはシュガースクラブを使わないようにしましょう。

4 Language Highlights

受動態

能動態の文型の目的語を主語にして「〜は…される」という文型で同じ内容を表すと、それを受動態といいます。

◇能動態

We send our messages.

主語　他動詞　目的語

◇受動態

Our messages　　　are sent　　　(by us).

能動態の文の目的語　be 動詞＋過去分詞　by ＋能動態の文の主語

◇現在形の受動態

These sugars are added to many popular foods and drinks.（本文第 3 段落）

時制が are で現在形になっています。一般的な内容なので、一般の人を表す by them（彼らによって）が省略されています。

◇過去形の受動態

Sugar was cultivated in India.（本文第 2 段落）

時制が was で過去形になっています。

◇未来形の受動態

The author's new book will be published next month.
（その著者の新著は来月出版されます）

時制が will be で未来形になっています。出版社によって出版されることは明らかであり、あまり重要ではないので by 〜は省略されています。

◇過去分詞が形容詞として用いられる例もある

制限用法：this increased use of sugar（本文第 1 段落）, processed foods（本文第 3 段落）, added sugar（本文第 4 段落）

叙述用法：was limited（本文第 2 段落）

Grammar Practice

次の日本語文に合うように英語文を完成させましょう。ただし文頭に来る語も小文字にしてあります。

1. ジャガイモは、のちに世界中で栽培されました。

the world / were / over / potatoes / cultivated / later / all

_____

2. その有名な温泉地は、多くの旅行者によって訪問されています。

famous / by / the / is / resort / hot spring / many tourists / visited

_____

3. 巨大な砂糖の大農園がヨーロッパ人によってカリビアンの島々に作られました。

sugar plantations / the / the Caribbean islands / were / on / by the
Europeans / huge / built

_____

4. 添加糖の入った加工食品は、健康によくない食品の例です。

processed / added / are / foods / sugar / unhealthy foods / with /
examples of

_____

5. 先進国では多くの砂糖が消費されています。

lot of / in / sugar / a / nations / consumed / is / developed

_____

5 Slash Reading Challenge 🎧 1-41

日本文の意味のかたまりに従って、英文にスラッシュ（ / ）を入れましょう。次に音声を聞い
て区切りごとに発話してみましょう。

1. 昔々／砂糖は贅沢品でした／お金持ち層だけが／金銭的余裕がありました

   Once upon a time, sugar was a luxury product that only the rich could
   afford.

2. サトウキビは／育ちます／暑くて湿度の高い地域で／多くの雨をともなって

   The sugarcane plant grows in hot, humid areas with lots of rain.

6 Let's Talk about It!

1. Discuss with your partners some of the reasons why eating too much sugar
   is an unhealthy habit.

2. Discuss with your partners why foods with natural sugar are better for
   your health than foods with added sugar.

Companion Animals

1 Vocabulary Gallery 🎧 2-01

以下のイラストを参考にして、英文の下線部の意味を枠内の選択肢より選んで記号（a 〜 f）で答えましょう。

① loneliness	② military	③ nursing home(s)
④ exam(s)	⑤ unsteady	⑥ harness(es)

1. <u>Loneliness</u> is a problem for people who have no friends. (　　)
2. Women and men can serve in the <u>military</u>. (　　)
3. Elderly individuals, especially if they are sick, often live in
   a <u>nursing home</u>. (　　)
4. Students feel stressed when they take an <u>exam</u>. (　　)
5. He uses a cane because his walking is <u>unsteady</u>. (　　)
6. Service dogs for the blind wear a <u>harness</u>. (　　)

a) 高齢者施設	**b)** 孤独	**c)** 試験
d) 不安定な	**e)** 軍隊	**f)** 引き具、装具

2 Warm-up Dialogue 🖸 2-02

動物学を専攻するティナがクラスメイトのヤスオに介助動物の重要性を説明しています。音声を聞いて、空欄に聞き取った英語を書きましょう。

Yasuo: I've noticed that lots of people in the US have pets. But there are also lots of service animals – (　　　　　) (　　　　　), animals that work.

Tina: That's right, Yasuo. These service animals have jobs – like with the military or with people who have health problems.

Yasuo: What kind of health problems? So how can service animals help?

Tina: In SO many ways! Like helping blind or deaf people, calming kids with autism, or giving emotional support to (　　　　　) (　　　　　) (　　　　　).

Yasuo: Just amazing! I didn't know that animals could learn to do so many great things.

Tina: Well, (　　　　　) (　　　　　) (　　　　　). For people with health problems, a service animal really improves the quality of their life.

> **Note**　**kids with autism:** 自閉症の子ども

Multiple Choice Questions

空欄に入る最も適切なものを選びましょう。

1. Yasuo is surprised that ＿＿＿＿＿＿ in the US.
   a. all animals are pets
   b. most pets are working animals
   c. there are many pets and many working animals

2. Tina tells Yasuo that service animals help ＿＿＿＿＿.
   a. people with health problems
   b. people who can see and hear
   c. people who love pets

3. Yasuo is surprised that ＿＿＿＿＿.
   a. service animals never work
   b. service animals can learn to do so many things
   c. service animals help only people with emotional problems

3 Ready to Read 🎧 2-03

Medical experts generally agree that animals are good for your health. Pets are wonderful, loyal companions, especially if you live alone. Playing with your pet or taking your furry friend on a walk
5 is great exercise. Pets help reduce loneliness and stress.

Not all animals are pets. Some dogs work with the police or military in specialized K-9 units. Others are certified *therapy animals*. Along with their owners, they visit patients in hospitals and nursing homes. Some colleges let
10 students interact with therapy animals during exam week. These visits help reduce anxiety in patients and students alike.

Some animals help individuals with serious health problems. These *service animals* are trained for months, even years, so they can assist people with important daily activities. Now let's look at some examples.

15 Guide dogs for the blind act as the "eyes" for someone who cannot see. Hearing dogs alert deaf individuals to important sounds. Diabetic alert dogs let the owners know when their blood sugar level is low. Autism assistance dogs calm children during an emotional crisis. Psychiatric service dogs give emotional support to patients suffering from PTSD or depression.

20 My friend Ralph has Parkinson's. Because of this degenerative disease, his balance is poor, and his walking is unsteady. But thanks to his wonderful service dog named Atlas, the quality of Ralph's life has improved.

After 18 months of training, Ralph and Atlas are a team. When walking, Ralph holds the handle on Atlas's harness. With this support, he feels safer
25 and more confident. Now the two "guys" really enjoy taking a walk and stopping to chat with friends.

Don't you agree that companion animals make us feel happy and healthy?

(Words: 278)

Notes   furry: 毛むくじゃらの   **psychiatric service dog**(s): 精神支援犬
diabetic alert dog(s): 糖尿病警告犬

Comprehension Check-up

本文の内容に合っている文には T を、合っていない文には F を [　] に記入しましょう。

1. Pets are wonderful, loyal companions that are good only for people who live alone.　[　　]

2. Therapy animals work with the military in specialized K-9 units.　[　　]

3. Service animals help individuals with serious physical or mental problems.　[　　]

4. When people with health problems have service animals, the quality of their life improves.　[　　]

Guided Summary　🎧 2-04

次の英文は本文を要約したものです。(1) から (8) の空所に、下の (a) 〜 (h) から適語を選んで記入し文を完成させましょう。

Medical (1)＿＿＿＿＿ agree that animals are good for your health. If you have a pet, you (2)＿＿＿＿＿ more, and you feel less stressed and less lonely. Not all animals are pets. Dogs in the K-9 unit work with the military. (3)＿＿＿＿＿ dogs visit patients in hospitals and (4)＿＿＿＿＿ homes. Service animals help people who are blind or deaf. They warn patients with (5)＿＿＿＿＿ when their blood sugar level is low. They calm (6)＿＿＿＿＿ children, give emotional support to patients with PTSD or (7)＿＿＿＿＿, and help people with degenerative (8)＿＿＿＿＿. Animals keep us happy and healthy.

Word List

(a) nursing	**(b)** experts	**(c)** autistic	**(d)** diseases
(e) exercise	**(f)** diabetes	**(g)** therapy	**(h)** depression

Did You Know?

アメリカ合衆国では、法律により介助動物はホテルでもレストランでも店でも、さらにバスや電車や飛行機まで、どこへでも飼い主に同伴することができます。介助動物の運賃は無料です。彼らは、飼い主の足元に静かに座り、仕事用の装具を身に付けなければなりません。また、介助動物は装具を身に付けている時、ペットのようにかわいがられるべきではありません。彼らは仕事中、自分の飼い主のニーズに応えるため、あらゆることに集中しなければならないのです。

4 Language Highlights

使役動詞など

本来「使役」というのは「誰かに何かをさせること」ですので、使役動詞というのは「（人）に～させる」という動詞（make, let, have）になりますが、それに加え help も「（人）を手伝って～させる」という解釈ができるので、ここでは使役動詞とあわせて扱います。
「make/let/have/help ＋人＋動詞の原形（原形不定詞)」の形で使います。

make

「強制的に、または、必然的に～させる」という意味です。

　Companion animals <u>make</u> us feel happy and healthy.（本文第 7 段落）

let

「（相手がしたがっていることを）～させてあげる」という意味です。

　Some colleges <u>let</u> students interact with therapy animals during exam week.
（本文第 2 段落）

　Diabetic alert dogs <u>let</u> the owners know when their blood sugar level is low.
（本文第 4 段落）

have

「（当然のことを）～させる、～してもらう」という意味です。

　I will <u>have</u> him wait at the station.（私は駅で彼を待たせておきます）

help

「（人を手伝って）～させる」「人が～するのを手伝う」という意味です。

　I <u>helped</u> him study English.（私は彼が英語を勉強するのを手伝いました）

目的語の「人」を伴わずに「help ＋原形不定詞」または「help ＋ to 不定詞」の形もあります。

　Pets <u>help</u> reduce loneliness and stress.（本文第 1 段落）

Grammar Practice

次の日本語文に合うように英語文を完成させましょう。ただし文頭に来る語も小文字にしてあります。

1. 私はあなたに試験の結果をお知らせします。

   the test / will / I / you / know / of / let / the result

   _____

2. 新しいウイルスの蔓延は私たちを家にとどまらせました。

   of / stay / the spread / home / made / the / new virus / us

   _____

3. 社長は彼の秘書にホテルの予約をさせました。

his / reservation / had / make / the president / a / secretary / hotel

_____

4. ペットは飼い主が日常生活からのストレスを減らすのを助けることができます。

help / from / pets / stress / can / reduce / the owners' / daily life

_____

5. 先生方は生徒たちに放課後とても一生懸命に勉強をさせました。

made / very / school / the students / the teachers / hard / study / after

_____

5 Slash Reading Challenge 🎧 2-05

日本文の意味のかたまりに従って、英文にスラッシュ（ / ）を入れましょう。次に音声を聞いて区切りごとに発話してみましょう。

1. ペットは素晴らしく／忠実な仲間です／特に／もしあなたが一人暮らしなら

   Pets are wonderful, loyal companions, especially if you live alone.

2. あなたのペットと遊ぶこと／あるいはあなたの毛むくじゃらの友を連れ出して散歩に行くのは／素晴らしい運動です

   Playing with your pet or taking your furry friend on a walk is great exercise.

6 Let's Talk about It!

1. Discuss with your partners why you would like, or why you wouldn't like, to have a pet.

2. In the US, service animals are quite common, but in Japan they are not so common. Discuss with your partners why the Japanese need or don't need more service animals to help individuals with serious health problems.

Chapter 10 Music And Medicine

1 Vocabulary Gallery 🎧 2-06

以下のイラストを参考にして、英文の下線部の意味を枠内の選択肢より選んで記号（a ～ f）で答えましょう。

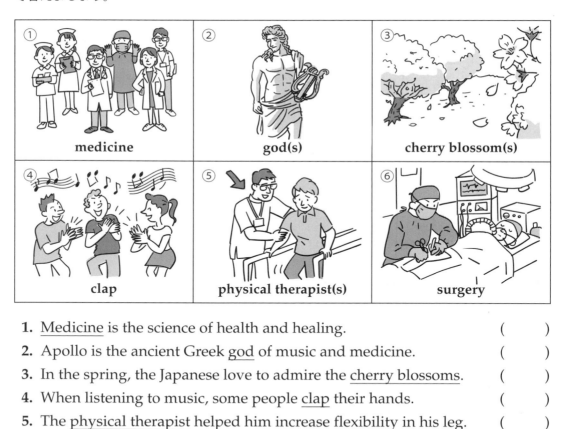

① medicine	② god(s)	③ cherry blossom(s)
④ clap	⑤ physical therapist(s)	⑥ surgery

1. <u>Medicine</u> is the science of health and healing. （　　）
2. Apollo is the ancient Greek <u>god</u> of music and medicine. （　　）
3. In the spring, the Japanese love to admire the <u>cherry blossoms</u>. （　　）
4. When listening to music, some people <u>clap</u> their hands. （　　）
5. The <u>physical therapist</u> helped him increase flexibility in his leg. （　　）
6. The boy needed <u>surgery</u> on his broken knee. （　　）

a) たたく	b) 神	c) 医学
d) 桜の花	e) 理学療法士、物理療法士	f) 手術

2 Warm-up Dialogue 🎵 2-07

ミズエは友人のデイヴに音楽と医学の関係を話しています。音声を聞いて、空欄に聞き取った英語を書きましょう。

Mizue: Hey, Dave. Did you know that the ancient Greeks had a special god for both music and medicine?

Dave: No, I didn't. (　　　　　) (　　　　　　　), I don't get the connection between the two.

Mizue: At first, I didn't, but now I understand why music is good for our body and our mind.

Dave: OK. I get the body part. I mean, music makes exercise more fun. But I don't get why music is good for our mind.

Mizue: Well, just think about how music affects your mood. Like a special song that (　　　　　) (　　　　　　) (　　　　　　) somebody special. Or a song that gives you hope.

Dave: (　　　　　) (　　　　　　) (　　　　　　) (　　　　　　　), Mizue. I guess that's why "Amazing Grace" is one of my favorite songs.

> **Note**　"Amazing Grace": イギリス出身のジョン・ニュートン（John Newton）作詞、作曲者不明の讃美歌

Multiple Choice Questions

空欄に入る最も適切なものを選びましょう。

1. Mizue learned that the ancient Greeks _____.
   a. had one god for music and another god for medicine
   b. understood the connection between music and medicine
   c. believed music was good only for the body

2. At first, Dave didn't understand _____.
   a. why music is good for the mind
   b. why music is good for the body
   c. why music makes exercise more fun

3. Dave tells Mizue that songs like "Amazing Grace" _____.
   a. make exercise more fun
   b. make us forget someone special
   c. give us hope

3 Ready to Read 🔊 2-08

Did you know that music and medicine
are inter-related? The ancient Greeks
understood the important connection
between the two. That's why they had one
5 god for both music and medicine.

Music is good "medicine" for the mind.
It releases the "feel-good" chemicals in our brain, and helps us relax. If
patients listen to music before surgery, their anxiety level is reduced. Medical
professionals often prescribe music therapy for individuals with dementia.

10 Music also affects our mood. Sometimes it awakens wonderful memories.
Our favorite love song reminds us of our first kiss. A traditional song like
"Sakura" makes us think about the special beauty of cherry blossom season.

Music also gives us hope in moments of despair. When we listen to the
magnificent melody of "Amazing Grace," we want to become a better person.
15 Other times, music makes us think about world problems. The "Ode to Joy" in
Beethoven's Ninth Symphony sends an inspiring message about freedom and
peace.

Let's not forget that music is also good "medicine" for the body. As we
listen, we move to the beat. We may nod our head, or clap our hands. We
20 may even stand up, swing our hips, and start to dance.

Various studies indicate that music with a good rhythm encourages us to
exercise more. Better still, we feel less tired because we are having fun. But if
the music is slow and calm, our energy level drops.

Today many physical therapists incorporate music in patients'
25 rehabilitation programs. Exercises for increasing muscle strength or
improving flexibility are generally boring and repetitive. But when done to
music, they are almost fun, so the patients make more progress.

The ancient Greeks were right. Music and medicine are indeed connected.

(Words: 285)

Notes
despair: 絶望、落胆   progress: 進展
repetitive: 繰り返しの

本文の内容に合っている文には T を、合っていない文には F を [   ] に記入しましょう。

1. Music releases the "feel-good" chemicals in our brain, and helps us be calmer and less anxious.   [   ]

2. Music is good for the body because it makes us move with the beat. [   ]

3. The best music for encouraging people to exercise more should be slow and calm.   [   ]

4. Many physical therapists believe that patients make greater progress when they exercise to music.   [   ]

Guided Summary 🔊 2-09

次の英文は本文を要約したものです。(1) から (8) の空所に、下の (a) 〜 (h) から適語を選んで記入し文を完成させましょう。

There is an important (1)_____ between music and medicine. Music is good "medicine" for the mind. It (2)_____ the "feel-good" chemicals in our brain, and helps us relax. It calms (3)_____ with dementia, and (4)_____ anxiety in patients before surgery. Music also affects our (5)_____. It awakens wonderful (6)_____, gives us hope, and makes us think about world (7)_____. Music is also good "medicine" for the body. When listening to music, we move our body to the beat. Exercise is more fun when we listen to music with a good (8)_____.

Word List

| (a) individuals | (b) mood | (c) rhythm | (d) connection |
| (e) reduces | (f) problems | (g) releases | (h) memories |

Did You Know?

あなたは、犬が音楽を好きなことを知っていましたか？　様々な研究によると、犬はソフトロックやクラシック音楽、そしてリラックスさせる効果があることからレゲエまでも好きとのことです。彼らは、ヘビーメタルのような強くてうるさいビートの音楽はあまり好きではありません。なぜなら、それは犬たちに緊張を与えるからです。もしあなたがあなたのペットのためにどんな音楽を流そうかわからない時は、犬のために作られた CD アルバムを一枚買ってみてはいかがでしょうか。

4 Language Highlights

接続詞

文中の語と語、句と句、そして、節と節を結びつける語を接続詞といいます。

◇等位接続詞

接続詞の前後の節が対等の関係になるもので、and, so, but, or, nor, for などがあります。

But when done to music, they are almost fun, <u>so</u> the patients make more progress.
（本文第 7 段落）

◇従位接続詞

節と節を結びつける働きをし、従位接続詞によって導かれる節を従属節、文の中心になる節を主節とします。

▶副詞節を導く接続詞
時、原因、理由、譲歩などを表す副詞節を導きます。

<u>If</u> patients listen to music before surgery, their anxiety level is reduced. （本文第 2 段落）

<u>When</u> we listen to the magnificent melody of "Amazing Grace," we want to become a better person. （本文第 4 段落）

<u>As</u> we listen, we move to the beat. （本文第 5 段落）

We feel less tired <u>because</u> we are having fun. （本文第 6 段落）

▶名詞節を導く接続詞

Various studies indicate <u>that</u> music with a good rhythm encourages us to exercise more. （本文第 6 段落）

Grammar Practice

次の日本語文に合うように英語文を完成させましょう。ただし文頭に来る語も小文字にしてあります。

1. もしあなたが彼の歌を聞いたら、あなたはきっとその歌手を好きになるでしょう。

   you / you / if / his song, / listen to / like / will surely / the singer

   _____

2. 今、寝なさい。そうしなければ、朝、早く起きられませんよ。

   bed / in the morning / you won't / or / early / go to / now, / get up

   _____

3. 今日は暑くなるようなので、たくさん水を飲みなさい。

   water / as / it is / drink / hot / supposed to be / today, / plenty of

   _____

4. 私はウィーンに行きたいです。なぜならばそれは音楽の都だからです。

to / because / I'd like / of music / Vienna / the capital / visit / it is

_____

5. 統計は、あなたが宝くじに当たる確率はかなり低いことを示しています。

the lottery / statistics / have / you / show / chances of winning / that / extremely low

_____

5 Slash Reading Challenge 📀 2-10

日本文の意味のかたまりに従って、英文にスラッシュ（ / ）を入れましょう。次に音声を聞いて区切りごとに発話してみましょう。

1. 古代ギリシャ人たちは／理解していました／大切な結びつきを／二つの間の

The ancient Greeks understood the important connection between the two.

2. それは放出します／「いい気持ちの」化学物質を／脳内に／そして、私たちがリラックスするのを助けます

It releases the "feel-good" chemicals in our brain, and helps us relax.

6 Let's Talk about It!

1. Tell your partners what you feel when you listen to your favorite music.

2. Discuss with your partners why music is important/not important for you.

Chapter 11

Please Listen to Me!

1 Vocabulary Gallery 2-11

以下のイラストを参考にして、英文の下線部の意味を枠内の選択肢より選んで記号（a 〜 f)
で答えましょう。

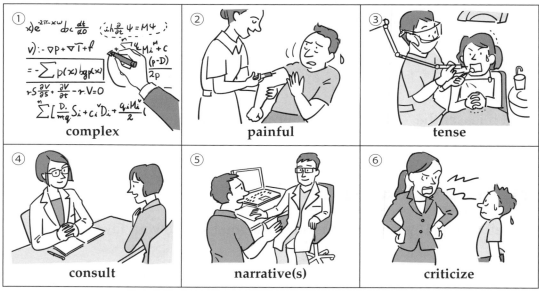

① complex	② painful	③ tense
④ consult	⑤ narrative(s)	⑥ criticize

1. The solution to his algebra equation is extremely <u>complex</u>.　(　　)
2. The flu injection was very <u>painful</u>.　(　　)
3. Every time I go to the dentist, I feel <u>tense</u>.　(　　)
4. Debbie <u>consulted</u> a therapist because of her emotional problems.　(　　)
5. The doctor listened to the patient's <u>narratives</u> about his health concerns.(　　)
6. The teacher <u>criticized</u> the boy's rude behavior.　(　　)

a) 複雑な	b) 相談する	c) 苦痛な
d) 批判する	e) 緊張した	f) 語り

2 Warm-up Dialogue CD 2-12

ヒロキは友人のデビーのことを心配しているようです。音声を聞いて、空欄に聞き取った英語
を書きましょう。

Hiroki: Hey, Debbie. You look really worried. What's wrong?

Debbie: (　　　　　) (　　　　　　　)! I'm so sad and depressed.

(　　　　　) (　　　　　), nobody wants to listen to my

problems.

Hiroki: Well, what about your friend Linda? Can't she help?

Debbie: Her! No way! Linda's so (　　　　　) (　　　　　)

(　　　　　) (　　　　　) that she has no time to listen to me.

Hiroki: Well, Debbie. Don't worry! I have time to listen. So just tell me

why you're so depressed.

Debbie: Oh, Hiroki, thanks SO much. You're really the best!

Note　**the best:** 最高（の人）

Multiple Choice Questions

1、3は空欄に入る最も適切なものを選びましょう。2は適切な答えを選びましょう。

1. Debbie is sad and depressed because _____.

　　a. she can't help Linda

　　b. she wants to listen to Hiroki

　　c. nobody wants to listen to her problems

2. Who is Debbie's real friend?

　　a. Linda

　　b. Hiroki

　　c. Both of them

3. Debbie tells Hiroki that he's the best because _____.

　　a. he knows that Debbie can help Linda

　　b. he offers to listen to Debbie's problems

　　c. he is Linda's friend

3 Ready to Read 🔵 2-13

Listening is an important and complex skill. Some say that listening is more difficult than speaking. They may be right because many people *hear* what you say but
5 don't *listen* to the real message in your words.

There are moments in life when you need to tell someone why you're sad or depressed. You want to release the painful emotions that are locked in your heart. You have to talk to someone who listens quietly, doesn't interrupt, and
10 doesn't criticize. After you "let go" of your negative feelings, you are less stressed and less tense.

Sometimes people cannot solve these emotional problems on their own, even when a good friend or a trusted family member is willing to listen. In such cases, they need to consult a therapist, a psychologist or perhaps a
15 psychiatrist. With these professional "listeners, " patients feel more relaxed, and talk more openly about their negative emotions.

Listening to patients should be part of every branch of healthcare, but unfortunately, this is not always the case. As medicine becomes more specialized, healthcare has become more impersonal. Some doctors don't have
20 time to listen. Others simply don't know how to listen. Gone are the days of personal care when the trusted family doctor listened to the patients' health concerns.

In recent years, many health professionals want to reverse this impersonal trend in medicine. They propose a personal, patient-oriented approach, which
25 they call *narrative medicine*. They listen as patients tell stories (narratives) about their health problems. In narrative medicine, doctors care for the patient as a person, not just a body.

Now you understand how listening can help you stay healthy.

(Words: 274)

Notes
lock: 閉じ込める
interrupt: さえぎる

impersonal: 非人間的な

Comprehension Check-up

本文の内容に合っている文には T を、合っていない文には F を [　] に記入しましょう。

1. Hearing what people say is not the same as listening to what they say.

   [　　]

2. When you are sad or depressed, you should always consult a "professional listener."

   [　　]

3. Today medicine is more specialized but also less personal. [　　]

4. In narrative medicine, health professionals listen as patients tell stories about their health problems.

   [　　]

Guided Summary 🎧 CD 2-14

次の英文は本文を要約したものです。(1) から (8) の空所に、下の (a) ～ (h) から適語を選んで記入し文を完成させましょう。

Listening is an important skill. When you feel sad or (1)_____, you should talk to a friend or a family member. You feel better after you "let go" of your (2)_____ feelings. If this does not help, you should (3)_____ a professional. Today medicine is more (4)_____ but less personal because most doctors don't listen to patients. Now many health professionals want to (5)_____ this trend. They (6)_____ a personal, patient-oriented approach called (7)_____ medicine. When physicians listen to patients' narratives, (8)_____ works better.

Word List

(a) specialized	(b) depressed	(c) narrative	(d) reverse
(e) negative	(f) healthcare	(g) propose	(h) consult

● Did You Know? ○

ある日、空腹のキツネは、カラスがくちばしに一切れのチーズをくわえ、木の高いところにとまっているのを見ました。キツネはそのチーズがほしかったので、カラスの美しい声を聞きたいと言いました。愚かなカラスはキツネのお世辞に耳を傾けました。カラスが歌い始めると、そのチーズは空腹のキツネの口の中に落ちていきました。時には、イソップがこの寓話で私たちに教えているように、耳を傾けるべきではない時を知ることは大切です。

4 Language Highlights

関係代名詞

◇関係代名詞の who, which, that

人あるいは物が、どのような人かあるいは物かを説明する場合に、関係代名詞 who, which, that などが使われます。

You want to release the painful emotions that are locked in your heart.（本文第 2 段落）

どんな感情（emotions）なのかを関係代名詞 that 以下が修飾しています。ここには that の代わりに which を使うこともできます。

You have to talk to someone who listens quietly.（本文第 2 段落）

どのような人（someone）であるのかを関係代名詞 who 以下で修飾しています。

◇関係代名詞の what

「先行詞＋関係代名詞」を一語で表す関係代名詞 what があります。

Many people hear what you say.（本文第 1 段落）

この what は、the thing(s) which と置き換えることができます。what you say で「あなたが言うこと」の意味です。

関係副詞

関係副詞は、接続詞の働きをするとともに、後ろに続く節に対しては動詞を修飾する副詞の働きをします。時を表す when、場所を表す where、理由を表す why、方法を表す how が主なものです。

There are moments in life when you need to tell someone why you're sad or depressed.（本文第 2 段落）

どういう時（moments）かを when 以下が説明しています。

Grammar Practice

次の日本語文に合うように英語文を完成させましょう。ただし文頭に来る語も小文字にしてあります。

1. 私は私の幸せな若い日々を思い出させてくれる古い歌が好きです。

   like / which / I / me / my happy young days / the old songs / remind / of

   _____

2. あなたは彼が言おうとしていることがわかりますか？

   what / you / do / say / trying / understand / he's / to

   _____

3. セラピストとは、あなたの語りを聞いてくれる専門職です。

to / a therapist / a professional / who / listen / your narratives / is / can

_____

4. あなたはあなたを憂鬱にする個人的な問題をいつでも私に話してくれていいですよ。

always / depressed / that / talk to me / your personal problems / you can / about / made you

_____

5. 放課後、子どもたちがお菓子を買って楽しむ近所の駄菓子屋の時代は過ぎ去ってしまいました。

of / gone are the days / when / buying snacks / neighborhood snack shops / enjoyed / kids / after school

_____

5 Slash Reading Challenge 🎧 2-15

日本文の意味のかたまりに従って、英文にスラッシュ（ / ）を入れましょう。次に音声を聞いて区切りごとに発話してみましょう。

1. これらの専門的な「聞き手」で／患者はよりリラックスした気分になります／そしてよりオープンに話します／彼らの否定的な感情について

   With these professional "listeners," patients feel more relaxed, and talk more openly about their negative emotions.

2. 近年／多くの医療専門職者たちは／くつがえしたいです／この非人間的傾向を／医学における

   In recent years, many health professionals want to reverse this impersonal trend in medicine.

6 Let's Talk about It!

1. Discuss with your partners why listening is such an important skill.

2. Discuss with your partners why you think that narrative medicine is/isn't a good way to improve healthcare in Japan.

Chapter 12

Let's Eat Together!

1 Vocabulary Gallery 🔊 2-16

以下のイラストを参考にして、英文の下線部の意味を枠内の選択肢より選んで記号（a ～ f）で答えましょう。

① snack(s)	② chat	③ table companion(s)
④ chew	⑤ controversial	⑥ smartphone(s)

1. She has gained weight because she eats too many unhealthy <u>snacks</u>. (　　　)
2. After school, I like to <u>chat</u> with my friends. (　　　)
3. My <u>table companions</u> talked about their trip to Italy. (　　　)
4. Your digestion will improve if you <u>chew</u> your food well. (　　　)
5. It's better to avoid discussing <u>controversial</u> topics like politics. (　　　)
6. It's impolite to use your <u>smartphone</u> in class. (　　　)

a) 噛む	**b)** スマホ	**c)** 共食者、一緒に食事をする人
d) 軽食、おやつ	**e)** おしゃべりする	**f)** 議論になるような

2 Warm-up Dialogue 🎧 2-17

大学のキャンパスを歩いていたフィルは友人のサトミに偶然会ったようです。音声を聞いて、空欄に聞き取った英語を書きましょう。

Phil: Hi, Satomi. I haven't seen you ( ) ( ). Where've you been?

Satomi: At my desk in my room! I've been working non-stop on the essay for my English class. It's been like more than a week.

Phil: You've gotta ( ) ( ) ( ), Satomi, otherwise you're gonna get sick. I bet you're not eating healthy food.

Satomi: You're SO right. I'm too busy to prepare healthy food, so I just ( ) ( ) on unhealthy snacks. Eating alone is so depressing.

Phil: Well, I'm going to help you out. I'm inviting you to have a healthy dinner with me. Meet me at my place at 7:00. OK?

Satomi: Great! Thanks so much, Phil, for the invite. Eating together is much more fun than eating alone. See you at 7:00.

> **Notes**
> **otherwise:** そうしなければ
> **invite:** (名) 招待

Multiple Choice Questions

空欄に入る最も適切なものを選びましょう。

1. Phil hasn't seen Satomi for a while because _____.
   a. she has been working on campus
   b. she has been writing an essay for her English class
   c. she has been sick for more than a week

2. Satomi has not been eating healthy because _____.
   a. she likes to pig out on unhealthy snacks
   b. she hates eating healthy food
   c. she has no time to prepare healthy meals

3. Phil invites Satomi to have dinner with him because _____.
   a. he hates eating alone
   b. he wants to read her essay
   c. he's worried about her health

3 Ready to Read 🎧 2-18

Eating good food is a healthy habit. "What" you eat is important, but don't forget that "how" you eat is equally important. Medical experts agree that people who eat in
5　the company of family or friends are generally healthier than those who eat alone. Now let's look at some of the reasons why.

　　Eating alone occasionally is OK, but on a regular basis, it can cause health problems. On the one hand, you may gain weight either because you eat too
10　much or you snack too much on unhealthy food. Weight gain puts you at greater risk for high blood pressure, high cholesterol or heart disease.

　　On the other hand, you may lose weight when you eat alone because you don't eat enough. You skip meals, or eat at irregular hours. Eating too little is also an unhealthy habit.

15　Eating a meal with family or friends is more fun than eating alone. You eat more slowly because you stop to chat with your table companions. Your digestion is better because you take time to chew your food. This social interaction puts you in a good mood as long as you avoid controversial topics like politics!

20　Eating together also means talking with the people at the table. When, however, you text your friends during meals, you might as well be eating alone. So please put away those smartphones, and talk to your table companions.

　　Who you eat with is also important. Conversation at the dinner table is especially important for families. Parents and children who talk during meals
25　usually have a better relationship. These family chats help children develop better communication skills.

　　So please remember that eating together with family or friends is good for your health!

(Words: 286)

Note **politics:** 政治

Comprehension Check-up

本文の内容に合っている文には T を、合っていない文には F を ［　］に記入しましょう。

1. Medical experts agree that people who eat alone are healthier than those
   who eat with family or friends. ［　］

2. People who eat alone always eat too much and gain weight. ［　］

3. Eating together means talking to your table companions, not texting your
   friends. ［　］

4. When parents and children talk at the dinner table, they generally have a
   better relationship. ［　］

Guided Summary 🎧 2-19

次の英文は本文を要約したものです。(1) から (8) の空所に、下の (a) ～ (h) から適語を選んで
記入し文を完成させましょう。

Medical (1)_____ agree that people who eat with family or friends are
generally (2)_____ than those who eat alone. Eating alone on a regular
basis can cause health problems such as (3)_____ gain, high blood
(4)_____, high cholesterol, heart (5)_____ or sometimes weight loss.
Eating together is more fun. Your (6)_____ is better because you eat slowly.
Eating together means talking with your table (7)_____, not texting friends.
It also helps improve the (8)_____ between parents and children. In short,
eating together is good for our health.

Word List

(a) disease	(b) experts	(c) digestion	(d) relationship
(e) weight	(f) companions	(g) healthier	(h) pressure

Did You Know?

"companion"（友だち、仲間）の語の元の意味は「共食する、一緒に食べる」と関係している
ということをあなたは知っていましたか？　その語は、ラテン語の companio に由来し、それ
は、パン（pan）をあなたとともに（com）食べる人、という意味です。したがって、companion
という語は、友だちを表します。なぜならば、一緒に食事をすることは友情の印だからです。
あなたも不快な人と一緒に食事をしたいとは思わないですよね？

4 Language Highlights

間接疑問文

文全体が疑問文である直接疑問文とは違って、疑問文が他の文の一部になっているものを間接疑問文といいます。

◇**直接疑問文**

Where do you go?（あなたはどこに行きますか？）

◇**間接疑問文**

I don't know where you go.（あなたがどこに行くのか私は知りません）

Do your parents know where you go?
（あなたの両親はあなたがどこに行くのか知っていますか？）

Where you go is very important.（あなたがどこに行くのかがとても重要です）

間接疑問文では、「疑問詞＋主語＋動詞」と平叙文の語順となります。

What you eat is important.（本文第1段落）

How you eat is equally important.（本文第1段落）

Who you eat with is also important.（本文第6段落）

Grammar Practice

次の日本語文に合うように英語文を完成させましょう。ただし文頭に来る語も小文字にしてあります。

1. 私は次に何が起こるのか想像できませんでした。

what / I / next / imagine / would / not / could / happen

_____

2. この病気の大流行がいつ終わるのか、誰もわかりません。

one / no / over / when / be / knows / will / this pandemic

_____

3. 私たちは、次のアメリカ合衆国大統領が誰になるのか予測できません。

can't / who / we / guess / the / next / US President / will be

_____

4. 彼女の母親は彼女が誰と遊ぶのかいつもチェックしています。

is / her mother / she / who / always / plays / checking on / with

_____

5. どのように話すかが、よい第一印象を形成するのに大切です。

in making / a / how / very important / good first impression / speak / you / is

_____

5 Slash Reading Challenge 🎧 2-20

日本文の意味のかたまりに従って、英文にスラッシュ（ / ）を入れましょう。次に音声を聞いて区切りごとに発話してみましょう。

1. 医学の専門家たちは同意します／食事をする人たちは／家族のいるところで／または友だち（のいるところで）／一般的により健康ということに／一人で食べる人たちよりも

   Medical experts agree that people who eat in the company of family or friends are generally healthier than those who eat alone.

2. まず／あなたは体重を増やすかもしれません／あなたは食べすぎるからか／あるいは、がつがつ食べすぎるからか／不健康な食べ物を

   On the one hand, you may gain weight either because you eat too much or you snack too much on unhealthy food.

6 Let's Talk about It!

1. Discuss with your partners why it's bad or why it's not bad to text while you are having dinner with family or friends.

2. Discuss with your partners the reasons why you think it's good or why you think it's bad to eat alone.

Chapter 13 Being Alone vs. Being Lonely

1 Vocabulary Gallery 🎵 2-21

以下のイラストを参考にして、英文の下線部の意味を枠内の選択肢より選んで記号（a ～ f）で答えましょう。

① alone	② goal(s)	③ nervous
④ aging population(s)	⑤ face-to-face	⑥ tweet(s)

1. She eats <u>alone</u> when she wants to relax.　　　　　　　　　　(　　)
2. Some people don't have any <u>goals</u> for their future.　　　　　　(　　)
3. Job interviews often make the candidates feel <u>nervous</u>.　　　　(　　)
4. The cost of healthcare increases in nations with <u>aging populations</u>.　(　　)
5. <u>Face-to-face</u> meetings are more fun than online ones.　　　　(　　)
6. Teachers get angry when students send <u>tweets</u> during class.　　(　　)

a) 人口の高齢化	**b)** ツイッターへの投稿	**c)** 一人で
d) 目標	**e)** 緊張した	**f)** 対面式の

2 Warm-up Dialogue 🎵 2-22

タカシは友人のエミリーに何やらアドバイスをしているようです。音声を聞いて、空欄に聞き取った英語を書きましょう。

Emily: Hey, Takashi! I need your advice. I'm really feeling down in the dumps these days. I'm just SO lonely.

Takashi: Emily, (   ) (   ) (   ) when you study abroad. You're far away from your family and friends. That's why you feel lonely.

Emily: So what should I do? Leave school here in Japan, and go back home?

Takashi: No way! You've gotta start making new friends here. I'm going to introduce you to my sister. She knows a lot of great people.

Emily: I'd love to meet her and her friends. Can you ask her (   ) (   ) (   ) so we can set up a time to meet?

Takashi: (   ) (   )! Now stop feeling so down in the dumps. Just think about all the fun you're going to have with your new friends. OK?

> **Notes**
> **down in the dumps:** 落ち込んで、悲しんで
> **study abroad:** 海外留学する

Multiple Choice Questions

空欄に入る最も適切なものを選びましょう。

1. Emily is down in the dumps because _____.
   a. she misses her family and friends
   b. she doesn't like her friends in Japan
   c. she is leaving school and going back home

2. Takashi tells Emily that it's natural to feel lonely when _____.
   a. you are a foreign exchange student
   b. you like the foreign country
   c. you like to have fun

3. Takashi tells Emily that the best way to stop feeling lonely is _____.
   a. for her to go home
   b. for her to study more
   c. for her to make new friends

3 Ready to Read 🔵 2-23

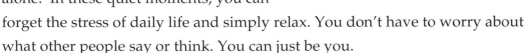

Did you know that there's a difference between *being alone* and *being lonely*? Please let me explain.

Sometimes it's good for you to be
5 alone. In these quiet moments, you can
forget the stress of daily life and simply relax. You don't have to worry about what other people say or think. You can just be you.

Psychologists agree that being alone – not all the time, of course – is a healthy habit. It helps you discover who you are so you can focus on your
10 goals for the future. It builds your self-confidence, and even increases your creativity. So don't be afraid of spending time alone!

Being lonely, on the contrary, is bad for your health because it makes you feel sad, nervous and even stressed. Lonely people often feel *down in the dumps*. Maybe they live far away from their family or friends. Maybe they don't like
15 their job or the place where they live.

Unfortunately the number of lonely people is on the rise, especially in countries with aging populations. Often elderly individuals who live alone don't have anybody to care for them. No wonder they feel lonely!

The Covid-19 pandemic has made everyone feel lonely and sad. After
20 months of lockdown, people want to have face-to-face meetings with family and friends. After all, FaceTime, texts and tweets cannot replace real-life social interaction.

In extreme cases, lonely people may become depressed. Then it's important for them to get help from healthcare professionals or government
25 social services.

Now I hope you understand the important difference between being lonely and being alone. Please take a little time from your busy schedule to be alone. That's a healthy habit.

(Words: 278)

Notes
Covid-19: 新型コロナウイルス感染症   **lockdown:** 都市封鎖
pandemic: 大流行   **FaceTime:** フェイスタイム（ビデオ通話用のアプリ）

本文の内容に合っている文には T を、合っていない文には F を [ ] に記入しましょう。

1. It's good for your health to spend lots of time alone.　[　]
2. Psychologists agree that we should be afraid of spending time alone.

　[　]

3. The pandemic has made people understand the importance of real-life
   social interaction.　[　]
4. When lonely people feel depressed, they should spend more time alone.

　[　]

Guided Summary　2-24

次の英文は本文を要約したものです。(1) から (8) の空所に、下の (a) 〜 (h) から適語を選んで
記入し文を完成させましょう。

There is an important (1)＿＿＿＿ between being alone and being lonely.
Spending some time alone is a healthy habit because you can forget the stress
of daily life and (2)＿＿＿＿. Being alone helps you (3)＿＿＿＿ on your
(4)＿＿＿＿ for the future. It also builds (5)＿＿＿＿, and increases your
creativity. Being lonely is bad for your health because it makes you feel down
in the dumps. The number of lonely people, especially since the (6)＿＿＿＿,
is on the rise. After months of (7)＿＿＿＿, people want to have (8)＿＿＿＿
meetings with family and friends.

Word List

(a) goals	(b) face-to-face	(c) pandemic	(d) focus
(e) self-confidence	(f) difference	(g) lockdown	(h) relax

Did You Know?

あなたの脳が休んで再び活性化するためには、一人の時間が必要であるということを知っていましたか？ しかし、一人の時間が長すぎることは、あなたの心身両面の健康にとってよくありません。ですから、信頼し尊敬する人たちと時間を過ごすことが重要なのです。困難に見舞われた時、あなたの友人がそばにいて、難局を乗り切る助けをしてくれるのです。

4 Language Highlights

it の特別用法

◇時間、天候、距離、明暗、温度などを表す文の主語となる

It is already time to finish now.（すでに終わる時間です）

It is raining today.（今日は雨が降っています）

It is really hot today.（今日は本当に暑いです）

◇形式主語［仮主語］として、後に来る真主語の不定詞句・that 節などを受ける

It's important for them to get help from healthcare professionals.（本文第 7 段落）

「It is 形容詞 for 人 to 不定詞」で「（人）にとって〜することは…である」という意味を表します。

It's sometimes sad when they live alone.

形式主語 it は when 節を表します。

It surprised us that he had finished the work in an hour or two.
（彼が 1 〜 2 時間でその仕事を終えてしまったことは、私たちを驚かせました）

形式主語 it は that 節を表します。

◇**It is 〜 that [who, which]**…で「…するのは〜である」と〜の部分にくるものを強調する強調構文

It was this pen that I gave him for his birthday.
（私が彼の誕生日にあげたのはこのペンでした）

It was と that の間にはさまれている this pen が強調されています。

Grammar Practice

次の日本語文に合うように英語文を完成させましょう。ただし文頭に来る語も小文字にしてあります。

1. 既に 4 時 30 分なので、私はこれをすぐに終えなければなりません。

   it's / soon / have / already 4:30, / I / to / and / finish this

   _____

2. その難しい試験に合格したことは、彼女にとって素晴らしいです。

   her / it's / for / difficult test / wonderful / pass / to / the

   _____

3. しっかりと手洗いをすることは、私たちにとってとても大切です。

important / it's / thoroughly / very / to / us / for / wash our hands

_____

4. あなたのいとこの葬式に出席できないのは悲しい状況です。

it's a / cannot / situation / when / your cousin's funeral / sad / you / attend

_____

5. 彼女を有名にしたのは、この本でした。

it / that / this / was / her / book / made / famous

_____

5 Slash Reading Challenge 🎵 2-25

日本文の意味のかたまりに従って、英文にスラッシュ（ / ）を入れましょう。次に音声を聞いて区切りごとに発話してみましょう。

1. あなたはする必要がありません／について心配する／他の人が何を言うか／または考える

   You don't have to worry about what other people say or think.

2. それはあなたが発見するのを助けます／あなたが誰であるか／だからあなたは焦点を当てることができます／あなたの目標に／将来の

   It helps you discover who you are so you can focus on your goals for the future.

6 Let's Talk about It!

1. Discuss with your partners why being alone sometimes is a healthy habit.

2. Discuss with your partners why you think technology can/can't replace real-life social interaction.

Chapter 14 — Believe in Yourself!

1 Vocabulary Gallery 🎧 2-26

以下のイラストを参考にして、英文の下線部の意味を枠内の選択肢より選んで記号（a 〜 f）で答えましょう。

① decision(s)	② direction(s)	③ choose
④ strength(s)	⑤ weakness(es)	⑥ unique

1. My <u>decision</u> was to study English instead of Spanish. （　　）
2. Your major in college will determine the <u>direction</u> for your future. （　　）
3. She usually <u>chooses</u> fish instead of pasta. （　　）
4. He's never late because punctuality is one of his <u>strengths</u>. （　　）
5. Eating too many desserts is one of her <u>weaknesses</u>. （　　）
6. Experts can identify individuals because fingerprints are <u>unique</u>. （　　）

a) 方向、方角	**b)** 独特な、唯一の	**c)** 短所、弱味、欠点
d) 決定、決心	**e)** 選ぶ、選択する	**f)** 長所、強味

2 Warm-up Dialogue 🎵 2-27

東京で働くリチャードは、友人のシノブに重要な決断について話しているようです。音声を聞いて、空欄に聞き取った英語を書きましょう。

Richard: Shinobu, I've gotta make a HUGE decision – one that will really change my future.

Shinobu: Why don't you tell me about it? Maybe I can help.

Richard: OK. You know that Junko and I are an item. Next month (　　　　) (　　　　) (　　　　) go home. So I have to decide whether to stay on here with her or return home alone.

Shinobu: Wow! That's a really big decision. But you have to choose what's best for YOU.

Richard: Yeah, but it's not so easy, especially when my family and some of my friends are telling me not to (　　　　) (　　　　) (　　　　) (　　　　).

Shinobu: Richard, don't listen to them. Just (　　　　) (　　　　) (　　　　), and then you'll make the right decision.

Note **an item:** (噂になっている) カップル

Multiple Choice Questions

空欄に入る最も適切なものを選びましょう。

1. Richard tells Shinobu that he has to decide whether or not _____.
   a. to get Junko an item
   b. to stay in Japan
   c. to go to the US with Junko

2. If Richard decides to stay in Japan and not return home, _____.
   a. his family will be happy
   b. nobody will be happy
   c. Junko will be happy

3. Shinobu tells Richard that _____.
   a. he should listen to the advice of his family and friends
   b. he must believe in himself
   c. he cannot make the right decision

3 Ready to Read 🎧 2-28

There are moments in life when you have to make important decisions – decisions that will determine the future direction of your life. Choosing which path
5 to follow is a real challenge. How do you know if you are making the right choice?

I can't tell you what to choose, but I can share with you the advice that my father gave me many years ago. "Believe in yourself," he told me, "and then you'll make the right decision for you." Now let me give you some hints about
10 how to believe in yourself.

The first and perhaps most important step is to *know yourself*. In other words, you have to recognize your strengths as well as your weaknesses. Maximize your good points, and minimize the bad ones. If you make a mistake, as we all do, admit it, and learn from what you did wrong. Accept
15 the consequences of your actions and choices.

The next step is to *like yourself*. This means remembering that you are unique and different from any other person in the world. Take pride in your special qualities, and don't try to be somebody else. Don't let social media control you. Never be afraid of being you!

20 Believing in yourself is not always easy. Sometimes you may doubt your own judgment, especially when family or friends tell you that you're making the wrong choice. But if you believe that your decision is the right one for you, don't listen to their advice. Live your life the way you want to – not the way others want you to.

25 When you believe in yourself, you have the power and energy to choose what is right for you. Then you can shape your future.

(Words: 286)

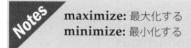
maximize: 最大化する
minimize: 最小化する

Comprehension Check-up

本文の内容に合っている文には T を、合っていない文には F を ［　］ に記入しましょう。

1. When you have to make an important decision, it's impossible to make the
   right choice. ［　　］
2. If you know yourself and like yourself, you can believe in yourself.
   ［　　］
3. You should always follow the advice that your family and friends give you.
   ［　　］
4. Believing in yourself gives you the power and energy to shape your future.
   ［　　］

Guided Summary 🎧 2-29

次の英文は本文を要約したものです。(1) から (8) の空所に、下の (a) ～ (h) から適語を選んで
記入し文を完成させましょう。

Sometimes you have to make (1)＿＿＿＿＿ decisions that determine the future
(2)＿＿＿＿＿ of your life. If you believe in yourself, you can make the right
(3)＿＿＿＿＿ for you. To believe in yourself, you must first *know yourself* –
your (4)＿＿＿＿＿ as well as your weaknesses. You must also *like yourself*, and
(5)＿＿＿＿＿ that you are (6)＿＿＿＿＿. Believing in yourself is not always easy,
especially when family or friends think your choice is wrong. But when you
believe in yourself, you have the (7)＿＿＿＿＿ and energy to make the right
decision and (8)＿＿＿＿＿ your future.

Word List

(a) recognize	(b) decision	(c) power	(d) important
(e) shape	(f) strengths	(g) unique	(h) direction

Did You Know?

19 世紀のイギリスの詩人ウィリアム・アーネスト・ヘンリー（1849-1903）がラテン語で「征服されない」という意味の Invictus という短い詩を書いたことを知っていましたか？　この詩の最終連で、彼は私たちの選択が私たちの未来を決定づけるのだということを思い起こさせてくれます。私たちは強くある必要があり、そして自分たちの選択に責任を持つ必要があります。ヘンリーの詩は、「私は私の運命の主人である。私は私の魂の主である。」という有名な言葉で幕を閉じます。

4 Language Highlights

「疑問詞＋ to 不定詞」は「〜すべきか、〜したらよいか」などの意味で、名詞句として主語や目的語や補語として用いられます。

◇主語として用いる例

How to start a class is always very important.
（授業をどのように始めるかは常に大切なことです）

◇目的語として用いる例

I can't tell you what to choose.（本文第 2 段落）

Let me give you some hints about how to believe in yourself.（本文第 2 段落）

上の例は、動詞 tell の目的語、下の例は、前置詞 about の目的語になっています。「疑問詞＋ to 不定詞」を目的語にとる動詞は、know, learn, teach, tell, show, ask, explain, remember, consider など知識を表す動詞です。

◇補語として用いる例

The question is who(m) to ask for advice.（問題は、誰に助言を求めるかです）

元来は、目的格の whom が用いられますが、口語では who も用いられます。

「whether ＋ to 不定詞 or ＋ to 不定詞」も「疑問詞＋ to 不定詞」の発展した形です。

Richard doesn't know whether to stay in Tokyo or to go home.
（リチャードは東京にとどまるべきか、帰国すべきかわかりません）

Grammar Practice

次の日本語文に合うように英語文を完成させましょう。ただし文頭に来る語も小文字にしてあります。

1. あなたのお名前をどのように発音するのか私に教えていただけますか？

   you / your name / could / to / me / tell / pronounce / how

   _____

2. その地震が起きた時、私はどうしたらよいのかわかりませんでした。

   the earthquake / what / when / I / happened, / to / didn't know / do

   _____

3. 彼は、京都に行くべきか家にとどまるべきかわかりませんでした。

   whether / or / he / didn't know / home / to Kyoto / to go / to stay

   _____

4. 夕食をどこに食べに行くかでいつも私たちはイライラします。

to / for / where / us / always / eat out / dinner / frustrates

_____

5. この職場で難しいのは、誰に助言を求めていいのかということです。

who / is / the difficulty / to / this workplace / ask for / advice / of

_____

5 Slash Reading Challenge 🎧 2-30

日本文の意味のかたまりに従って、英文にスラッシュ（ / ）を入れましょう。次に音声を聞いて区切りごとに発話してみましょう。

1. これは意味します／覚えていることを／あなたは独特で／そしてほかのどの人とも
   違っているということを／世界中の

   This means remembering that you are unique and different from any
   other person in the world.

2. あなたの人生を生きてください／あなたが望むように／ようではなく／他人があなた
   に望む

   Live your life the way you want to – not the way others want you to.

6 Let's Talk about It!

1. Discuss with your partners why it's really important to *like yourself*.

2. Discuss with your partners the decision that Richard and his girlfriend
   Junko have to make.
   a. Why should/shouldn't Richard stay in Japan?
   b. Why should/shouldn't Junko move to the USA?
   c. Why should/shouldn't they break up?

Chapter 15
The Interview

1 Vocabulary Gallery

 2-31

以下のイラストを参考にして、英文の下線部の意味を枠内の選択肢より選んで記号（a ～ f）で答えましょう。

① co-author(s)	② timely	③ precious
④ cherish	⑤ knowledge	⑥ investment(s)

1. When two people write a book together, they are <u>co-authors</u>.　(　)
2. Thanks to the <u>timely</u> hurricane warning, everybody was prepared.　(　)
3. This diamond ring is very <u>precious</u>.　(　)
4. I will always <u>cherish</u> the photos you gave me.　(　)
5. His <u>knowledge</u> of computer programming is impressive.　(　)
6. What is a better <u>investment</u> – stocks or gold?　(　)

a) 大切な、大事な	b) 投資	c) 共著者
d) 大切にする	e) 知識	f) 時機を得た、適時の

2 Warm-up Dialogue 🎵 2-32

ヨーコは友人のピーターにジョアニー・マッコーネル博士へのインタビューについて話しています。音声を聞いて、空欄に聞き取った英語を書きましょう。

Yoko: Hey, Peter. I've got some amazing news. I'm going to do an interview with Dr. McConnell for our school paper.

Peter: That's awesome, Yoko! Have you prepared all your questions?

Yoko: Of course, but I'm SO nervous about interviewing her. What's she like ( ) ( )?

Peter: Low key and easy to talk to, so don't worry. By the way, everybody calls her Dr. Joanie. She prefers that.

Yoko: Well, that makes me feel a little less nervous. But what if I make a mistake in English? Will she ( ) ( )?

Peter: No way! She'll be impressed that you're interviewing her in English. After all, that's your second language, so don't get uptight about making a mistake. ( ) ( ) ( ).

> **Notes**
> **awesome:** すごい、素晴らしい
> **low key:** 控えめな
> **get uptight:** 緊張して

Multiple Choice Questions

空欄に入る最も適切なものを選びましょう。

1. Yoko is nervous about the interview because _____.
   a. she hasn't prepared the questions
   b. she hasn't met Dr. Joanie in person
   c. she will be speaking Japanese

2. Peter tells Yoko that it's easy to talk to Dr. Joanie because _____.
   a. she is emotional
   b. she is low key
   c. she lost her key

3. When Japanese students speak to Dr. Joanie in English, _____.
   a. she gets mad if they make a mistake
   b. she tells them to speak in Japanese
   c. she is happy that they are speaking to her in English

3 Ready to Read 🎧 2-33

Yoko: Good morning, Dr. Joanie. My name is Yoko. I'd like to ask you a few questions about your new textbook. First of all, why did you
5   decide to write about health?

Dr. Joanie: Yoko, that's a very good question. My co-author Professor Yamauchi and I agree that health is a very timely topic. Today more and more people are concerned about the increase of serious health problems – obesity, high blood pressure, diabetes, heart
10   issues and loneliness. A healthy lifestyle can significantly reduce such risks. Health is a precious gift that we should cherish and not take for granted. Far too often, we appreciate good health only when we get sick.

Yoko: I agree. Now here's my second question. Why is it imperative,
15   especially for young people, to learn more about healthy habits?

Dr. Joanie: A famous saying reminds us that knowledge is power. That's true, particularly for something as important as health. When young people learn about healthy habits, the quality of their life will improve, both in the present as well as in the future.
20   Unfortunately some young people don't think about the future. They want to enjoy what's happening today, so they forget about what could happen tomorrow. That's a big mistake!

Yoko: You're so right, Dr. Joanie. Now can you give us some final words of advice?

25 **Dr. Joanie:** Of course! Healthy habits are a great investment for your future. Take good care of your body – healthy food, lots of water, exercise and enough sleep. And don't forget to take good care of your mind – positive thinking, trustworthy friends and believing in yourself.

30 **Yoko:** Thanks so much for your awesome message.

Dr. Joanie: Thanks to you, Yoko. You did a great interview!

(Words: 288)

Note   **take for granted:** 当たり前に思う

本文の内容に合っている文には T を、合っていない文には F を [ ] に記入しましょう。

1. Many people are worried because today there are more serious health
   problems than in the past.   [   ]
2. Healthy habits can help reduce your risks of serious diseases.   [   ]
3. Some young people prefer to focus on the present rather than the future.
                                                                  [   ]
4. A healthy lifestyle is a great investment for your future.   [   ]

Guided Summary 🎧 2-34

次の英文は本文を要約したものです。(1) から (8) の空所に、下の (a) ～ (h) から適語を選んで
記入し文を完成させましょう。

Health is a timely (1)_____ because today more and more people are
concerned about the (2)_____ of serious health problems. A healthy
(3)_____ can help reduce such (4)_____. We should always remember
that health is a (5)_____ gift, not to be taken for granted. That's why
everybody, especially young people, should learn about healthy habits. In this
way, we can (6)_____ the (7)_____ of our life in both the present and
the future. After all, healthy habits are a great (8)_____ for our future. So
let's take good care of our body and our mind!

Word List

(a) risks	(b) quality	(c) precious	(d) topic
(e) investment	(f) increase	(g) improve	(h) lifestyle

Did You Know?

あなたは、人間同士の触れ合い不足である「スキンシップ不足」（skin hunger）が心身両面の
健康によくないことを知っていましたか？　それは、人の免疫システムを弱める可能性があり、
また特に一人暮らしの人に、心理的問題を引き起こす要因にもなり得ます。多くの専門家が、ソー
シャルディスタンスが将来にわたっても続けられたら、より多くの人がこのような状態になる
だろうと警鐘を鳴らしています。

4 Language Highlights

Chapter 15 の文章中、下記 Chapter 1 ～ Chapter 14 までの Language Highlights の文法内容を探し、下線を引きチャプター番号を記してみましょう。

Chapter 1　　◆ when
Chapter 2　　◆現在形・過去形・現在完了形
Chapter 3　　◆ why
Chapter 4　　◆動名詞
Chapter 5　　◆前置詞
Chapter 6　　◆不定詞
Chapter 7　　◆比較級
Chapter 8　　◆受動態
Chapter 9　　◆使役動詞
Chapter 10　◆接続詞
Chapter 11　◆関係代名詞・関係副詞
Chapter 12　◆間接疑問文
Chapter 13　◆ It の特別用法
Chapter 14　◆疑問詞＋ to 不定詞

Grammar Practice

次の日本語文に合うように英語文を完成させましょう。ただし文頭に来る語も小文字にしてあります。

1. 私はあなたに教科書の書き方について 2、3 の質問をしたいと思います。

how / I'd like to / a few questions / ask / to write / a textbook / you / about

_____

2. 第一に、なぜあなたは日本に来る決心をしたのですか？

did / you / why / Japan / first of all, / come / to / decide to

_____

3. 今日では、ますます多くの人たちがその感染症の広まりを心配しています。

people / today / the infection / the spread / more and more / concerned about / of / are

_____

4. 若さは、若い人たちが大切にしなければならない大切な贈り物です。

a / should / precious gift / youth / that / cherish / is / young people

_____

5. 私たちは落ち込んだ時に、幸せをありがたく思います。

happiness / down / feel / we / we / in the dumps / appreciate / when

_____

5 Slash Reading Challenge CD 2-35

日本文の意味のかたまりに従って、英文にスラッシュ（／）を入れましょう。次に音声を聞いて区切りごとに発話してみましょう。

1. あまりにもしばしば／私たちは健康をありがたく思います／時にのみ／私たちが病気になる

   Far too often, we appreciate good health only when we get sick.

2. 若い人たちが健康的な習慣について学ぶ時／彼らの生活の質は／改善します／両方で、現在／と同様、未来においても

   When young people learn about healthy habits, the quality of their life will improve, both in the present as well as in the future.

6 Let's Talk about It!

1. Discuss with your partners why it's important, especially for young people, to learn about healthy habits.

2. Discuss with your partners what you like most about this textbook.

TEXT PRODUCTION STAFF

edited by	編集
Takashi Kudo	工藤 隆志

cover design by	表紙デザイン
Nobuyoshi Fujino	藤野 伸芳

illustrated by	イラスト
Yoko Sekine	関根 庸子

CD PRODUCTION STAFF

narrated by	吹き込み者
Karen Haedrich (AmE)	カレン・ヘドリック (アメリカ英語)
Howard Colefield (AmE)	ハワード・コールフィールド (アメリカ英語)

Healthy Habits for a Better Life
よりよい健康生活を求めて

2021年1月10日　初版発行
2023年9月10日　第4刷発行

著　者　Joan McConnell
　　　　山内　圭

発行者　佐野　英一郎

発行所　株式会社 成美堂
　　　　〒101-0052　東京都千代田区神田小川町3-22
　　　　TEL 03-3291-2261　FAX 03-3293-5490
　　　　https://www.seibido.co.jp

印刷・製本　　倉敷印刷株式会社

ISBN 978-4-7919-7229-6　　　　　　　　　Printed in Japan